BLOOD BROTHER

BLOOD BROTHER

33 Reasons My Brother Scott Peterson Is Guilty

ANNE BIRD

HARPER

NEW YORK · LONDON · TORONTO · SYDNEY

The names of certain individuals included in this book have been changed to protect their privacy.

Photography credits
All photographs courtesy of the author except: p. 113, AP Photo/Paul Sakuma; p. 135, AP Photo/*Modesto Bee*/Al Golub, pool; and p. 185, AP Photo/Ben Margot.

BLOOD BROTHER

Designed by Richard Ljoenes

Library of Congress Cataloging-in-Publication Data has been applied for.

ISBN 0-06-085033-7

07 08 09 WB/RRD 10 9 8 7 6 5 4 3 2

For Dr. Linda Tucker, who helped me find my way

CONTENTS

At my wedding, August 28, 1999: My brother Don, me, and Jackie, John, and Scott Peterson

JACKIE

O n a quiet midweek afternoon in early June 1997, I received a phone call that almost destroyed my life.

"Is this Anne Grady?" the caller asked. It was a man's voice, unfamiliar.

"Who is this, please?"

"My name is Don," he said. "You don't know me, but I'm related to you."

I immediately knew who he was. As an adopted child, this was the day I had been praying for, and dreading, my entire life. I was about to meet my biological family, and that family included three brothers I hadn't even known existed.

One of those brothers was Scott Peterson.

• • •

At the time of that fate-changing call, I was working at Cubic Corporation, a defense contractor in San Diego. Cubic does a lot of work for the U.S. government, and my father, Tom Grady, was president of Cubic Videocomm, the firm's high-tech division. Only two months earlier, in late May, I had been living in San Francisco, but I had a job I didn't like, no boyfriend, and a landlord who suddenly decided to double my rent.

So I returned home to Point Loma, in San Diego, to stay for a while with my parents, the people who adopted me at birth. I was adopted in 1965, when I was just a few days old; my brother Stephen was adopted three years later. My mother had been diagnosed with cancer, and she'd been told it was unlikely she'd ever have children, but five years after Stephen came along she became pregnant with her first child, Susan, and three years after that she gave birth to a son, Michael.

We lived in San Diego until I was twelve. Our parents loved all four of us equally. They had led a charmed life long before we came along. My father got his BA at Berkeley and his MBA from Harvard. After he graduated he became a navy officer and was stationed in San Diego. My mother, Jerri, was a teacher in landlocked Galesburg, Illinois, but she had a yen for the Pacific. One day she was talking to recruiters about teaching jobs out west, and when they mentioned San Diego she jumped at the chance. It was a good job, and San Diego was a navy base; she thought she might meet a man in uniform. As it turned out, she was right. One sunny afternoon not long after she settled in Mission Beach, she saw a tall, tanned, handsome man strolling past with a surfboard under his arm. He was exactly the kind of man she had hoped to meet, so she had the good sense to invite him to dinner. They were married in 1960.

Not long afterward, she was diagnosed with Hodgkin's disease. They got through it, however, and they even found a way to deal with the news that they might never have children of their own.

"You can adopt," the doctor said.

"Where would we start?" my father asked.

"I think I may know someone," the doctor replied.

He *did* know someone. He had a patient called Jackie Latham. She was unmarried and pregnant for the second time, and once again she didn't feel capable of caring for the child. The doctor told her about my parents' desire to adopt, and Jackie was tempted because the doctor described them as terrific, salt-of-the-earth type of people. When she heard about my mother's illness, she nearly changed her mind. She didn't want to give her little girl to someone who might not be around to care for her. But my father sent word back through the doctor that, if anything happened to Jerri, he was both willing and able to care for me by himself. Reassured, Jackie handed me over.

When I was six years old, my parents told me I was adopted. They explained that my mother, a nice lady, had felt ill equipped to care for me, that they had wanted a little girl just like me, and that they felt very lucky to have found me. I wasn't sure I understood what they meant, but I wasn't at all troubled by it. As far as I was concerned, they were my parents and always would be.

I never felt strange, different from, or less loved than other children, and I remember only one occasion where my history had any impact on me. I was in second grade at the time, and the class had been festooned with flags from many countries. We were told to stand under the flag of the country of our ancestors, and of course I had no idea where to go. When I noticed a large crowd under the British flag, I just joined in, and no one objected. There was safety in numbers.

When I went home I told my parents what had happened and asked them if they knew anything about my ancestry. "Well," my father said, "from what I recall, your mother had a little French and English on her mother's side and some German on her father's side."

"So did I stand in the right place?"

"You sure did," my mother said.

My parents are very grounded people. They have been married for almost forty-five years and have lived in the same house for nearly all that time. They seldom argue, they love to travel, and they're still friends with most of the people they knew when they were first married. In short, they are solid, reliable, and steady, and I can talk to them about anything.

I had a comfortable childhood, which bordered on privileged. We went on many vacations. We took road trips all up and down California—the beaches, the deserts, and the mountains—and often traveled to Mexico. We also went to Berkeley from time to time, to visit my paternal grandparents, and we loved to visit San Francisco. We also loved visiting my mother's parents in Illinois. In March we'd go to Yuma, Arizona, to watch the Padres play. My father bought some lemon groves there; to this day he refers to that investment as his one big lemon. Sometimes we'd have to go back to Arizona in July, at the height of the summer, to check on his lemony investment, and all I remember from those trips is the almost unendurable heat. To compound matters, my father didn't believe in air conditioning. "Roll down the window," he'd say. "Feel that fresh air!"

When I was nine, my mother discovered, to her great surprise, that she was pregnant, and a short while later my little sister, Susan, came along. I adored her. I treated her as my own personal doll and insisted on helping my mother with absolutely every aspect of child rearing. By the time Michael showed up two years later, I was less interested in changing diapers, and he didn't get anywhere near the attention I showered on Susan. I've been trying to make up for it ever since. But we all got along beautifully; we were a big, happy family, and each one of us was treated as special. I couldn't have asked for better or more loving parents, and as a result it was years before I became even mildly curious about my biological family.

My mother's sister Judi lived next door with her husband, Al; her other sister, Janice, lived a few blocks away with her husband, Larry. My mother had urged her sisters to move out west from Galesburg, tempting them with stories about handsome navy officers, and before long they were both living in San Diego with officers of their own.

Judi and Al had two daughters, Marci and Kristi, one of them a year older than me and the other a year younger. They couldn't have planned it any better. I was surrounded by wonderful, loving people.

I loved my life. I was always happy, almost relentlessly so.

• • •

When I was twelve, our family moved to England. My father's company had started a division in London, and he was asked to be the managing director, which is the British equivalent of a CEO.

As soon as we arrived, my parents bought a manor house just south of London, in Dorking, Surrey. The Cedars, as it was called, had three kitchens, two living rooms, various sitting rooms, a library, six bedrooms, a conservatory, and an outdated bell system to summon the servants that was great for playing hide-and-seek. Our neighbor told us that the Cedars was a "proper British house, complete with ghost." He said the ghost was actually the original owner of the house and assured us that she was a nice ghost, but we were still a little freaked out. Thankfully, none of us ever saw her.

We were always discovering new and unknown places at the Cedars, especially in the basement, which was damp and smelled of coal and was great fun to hide in. The yard was enormous, with a large fountain in the center and roses erupting in every direction. There was also a vegetable garden at the very back, with actual, growing vegetables, and a little outhouse tucked at the property's farthermost corner. However, the outhouse was surrounded by stinging nettles, so it was a little tricky to use.

It was a fascinating place and an interesting time. My mother hired a nanny to help with the two younger kids, with the garden, and with the shopping. This was a long way from Southern California. There were no tortillas with melted cheese. In their place were boiled potatoes and "mystery meat," as well as scones and other pastries. I didn't miss home, but I sure missed the food.

In September my parents sent to me a finishing school, and it almost finished me off. The following year, I transferred to the American Community School, which was just like the schools at home, only better. We were happy expatriates, enjoying life abroad. Many of the kids around me were from Texas, and their parents were in the oil business; for a while there I think I picked up a bit of a twang.

In my junior year, we returned to San Diego. I found myself attending classes at Point Loma High School with some of the same kids I had known four years earlier. It was as if I had never left. I was me again, but an enriched version of me, with four years' worth of incredible experiences behind me.

One day, I found myself at the San Diego Public Library—I'd come with my lifelong friend Jim, who had some research to do—and as I wandered around, bored, I found myself in front of the California Room. There was a sign next to the door that read, "Birth Records, Death Records, Marriage Records."

I knew my birth mother's name, Jacqueline Latham, and I was curious, so I went in and one of the employees directed me to the correct filing cabinet, then parked me in front of one of those ancient microfiche machines and showed me how to use it. There I discovered that Jacqueline Latham was married to Lee Peterson, and that they had two children, and the moment I saw that there were other children involved I stopped looking for more. My birth mother had another family now, and I had no business poking my nose into her life. Plus, I'd heard enough stories about adopted kids showing up unannounced on their birth parents' doorsteps, and these stories didn't always have happy endings. I didn't want to be part of someone's unhappy ending.

Still, I was growing more curious about my background. How

could I not be? As an adopted child, you wonder about everything. Was my mother a nice person? Why did she give me up? Did I look like her?

Sometimes, as I made my way through the world, I'd see someone who looked a little like me, or walked a little like me, and I'd think, *Are we related?*

And of course even at home anyone could see that neither Stephen nor I looked even remotely like our parents, while the two younger kids—tall, thin, attractive—could have passed for clones. Then again, I wasn't quite as exotic-looking as Stephen. He was 100 percent Italian, and his story is a lot more interesting than mine. His real grandfather, Midge Renault (his real name was Salvatore Annunziato), was a ruthless mobster on the East Coast, but he crossed the wrong people and got tossed off a bridge. His son, Stephen's father, was also in the mob, and when his mistress became pregnant she ran off, fearing for her life. She ended up in San Diego, at her aunt's house, and six months later little Stephen showed up at our place.

Stephen and I are very close, in part because we're both adopted, and throughout our lives we have always looked out for each other.

• • •

I went to Pine Manor College, an all girls' school in Chestnut Hill, near Boston, and got a BA in communications. Then I went back to England and spent a summer at Oxford University.

When I returned to the States, I found a job in public relations at the Golden Door, a family-owned spa in Escondido, not far from San Diego. They also own another spa in Tecate, Mexico, and I was always shuttling between the two. I loved my job. I met a great number of celebrities, but I won't name names.

When I started working there, both spas were operating well

below occupancy. By the time I left, you couldn't get in during the high winter season, and I was very proud of myself.

I also fell in love while working at the spas. Or I *thought* I fell in love. The marriage lasted eight months. I'm less proud of that.

I moved to San Francisco shortly thereafter and got into investment banking. Working with money was a lot less interesting than working with people, and when my landlord told me that my rent was about to double I took it as some kind of sign—don't ask me *what* kind of sign—and went back home.

There had been a guy in San Francisco, Tim Bird, but I was getting mixed signals from him, and after my bad marriage I was in a cautious mood—perhaps overly cautious. Tim and I went out a few times, and I enjoyed his company, but I wasn't sure if it was going anywhere, so I didn't wait around to find out if I was wrong.

Now here I was back in San Diego, working for my father, on that fateful June afternoon that altered the course of my life. I got two calls in quick succession. The first was from Stephen, who was calling from home.

"Some guy just called who thinks he's related to you!" he said. He was excited. Stephen has that underlying curiosity about who you are and where you came from that so many of us adopted kids have; it isn't something that ever goes away. The thing about it is that it's less fun to do the looking; you'd rather be found. You want to think that there's someone out there who abandoned you and still cares about you and wants to explain everything and answer every question. That's the dream. To have to do the looking yourself, only to run the risk of finding that maybe you're not wanted after all, that you're not even welcome—well, that's a pretty scary prospect. You can live with the feeling that your mother didn't love you enough to keep you, but it would be too hard to survive making it to adulthood and finding her only to be turned away.

"Did he leave a name?" I asked, a little wary.

"No," Stephen said. "But I gave him your number at work."

At that moment, I saw that my other line was flashing. I said good-bye to Stephen and reached for the flashing line.

"Hello?"

"Is this Anne Grady?" the man asked.

"Who is this, please?"

"My name is Don," he said. "You don't know me, but I'm related to you."

"Oh?"

"I was born two years before you, on April 2, 1963, and we share the same mother. She actually lives in Morro Bay, up the coast a ways, but she has a lot of family in San Diego."

"Oh my gosh," I said. I didn't know what else to say. I felt a little winded, to be honest, and Don sensed this, so he talked a little about himself. He told me that he lived back east, that he worked in the airline industry, and that he was married and had three kids.

"I was out in San Diego last year, and I met our mother, Jackie Latham, and it was a really wonderful experience. She's married now and has a couple of boys. I don't want to just drop all of this on you, though. I want you to have time to absorb it."

"I knew she was married," I said.

"Really?"

"I once saw her name in the county records. She was married to somebody named Lee Peterson." I was surprised that the name had stayed with me.

"That's right," he said. "I'd like to come out and meet you sometime. And I'd love for you to meet Jackie. But I don't want to be pushy here. I want you to take your time and think about this and let me know how you feel."

I didn't know how I felt, so I let him talk for a while and realized that his situation was very different from mine. Both of his parents had died, and he was estranged from his sister, who was also adopted. He had been seriously motivated to find his biological family because—outside of his wife and three children—he had absolutely no one else. I, however, had a wonderful, caring family, and I had always felt I belonged. Don was alone in the world; I had always been encircled by love.

"I don't know," I said. "I'm not sure about this."

"I'd be surprised if you were," he said. "It's a big step. But you should know that Jackie and Lee are terrific people. They have two wonderful sons together, and Lee has a couple of children from a previous marriage. They are a really great family."

"Okay," I said. "I'll think about it."

He gave me his various phone numbers, and I hung up. I felt like I had vertigo; the world around me seemed oddly muted out. The woman in the next cubicle had just poked her head over the partition, and she was bubbling over with excitement, telling me that some cute guy had answered her ad in the personals, and that they were about to arrange a date. I caught only half of what she said and sort of nodded at the appropriate intervals, trying hard to smile, but I felt like I was under water. I finally excused myself and made my unsteady way into my father's office.

"I just got this really amazing call," I said.

"Yeah?"

"This man from Pennsylvania says he's related to me."

"Really?" he asked.

"Yeah."

My father is not a guy who gets easily excited, and sometimes he can seem a little distant. In fact, sometimes he *is* a little distant, but that's just his manner; his heart is in the right place.

"That's really interesting," he said, but not exactly with unbridled enthusiasm.

When I got home, I told my mother about the call. I had this whole big family living right here in California, all up and down the coast, and suddenly I was very curious about them.

"I wonder if I look like my mother," I said.

"I wouldn't know," my mother said, but she said it with feeling, with enthusiasm even. "I never saw her."

"Not even when you picked me up at the hospital?"

"I didn't pick you up," she said. "We sent Aunt Judi and Uncle Al."

"What did they say about her? Did they say what she looked like?"

"Judi didn't remember much," my mother replied. "But Al said she had amazing legs."

"That's it? A pair of legs?!"

"I'm sorry," my mother said, laughing, and I laughed right along with her. "That's the whole story. It's all I have."

"What should I do?" I asked.

"What do you want to do?"

"I don't know," I replied. "But I'm curious. I'm thirty-two years old, and I've got to admit it: I am really very curious."

"Maybe you should talk to her," my mother said. "What's the worst that could happen?"

Plenty. But neither of us knew it then.

. . .

The next day, I called Don. I told him I was thinking about it and to give me a little time, and he was a perfect sweetheart. He said again that he hoped his call hadn't been too much of a shock, and he assured me that he would respect my decision, whatever it was. He also took the time to fill in a little more of the picture: "The two other kids, the boys she kept, they're called John and Scott. John's the rowdy one, but Scott is the golden boy. You'll know what I mean the moment you see him. You'll really like him."

A few days later, I called Don back and told him to give Jackie my number at work. She phoned the following day, and I could hear her walking around, pacing, as if she were nervous.

"Hi," she said. "I'm Jackie."

"Hi," I said.

She asked me what I looked like, and I tried to describe myself: petite, five feet four, shapely. (That was seven years ago, before marriage and two kids.)

"What color are your eyes?" she asked.

"Sort of greenish brown."

"Do you have the kind of eyelids you can put makeup on?"

I thought that was an odd question, but I told her yes.

"All the Lathams have nice eyes," she said.

"I hope that includes me," I said.

She asked me what I did. I told her I was working for my father, temporarily, and that I was planning on returning to San Francisco sometime soon.

"Do you have brothers and sisters?"

"Yes," I said. "Three." I gave her their names and their ages.

"You know," she said, "I've always wondered about you."

There was an awkward silence. I think I was kind of hoping for an explanation—why she left me, some details about her life, or how it felt to be talking to the little girl she'd given up—but it didn't come.

"I hope we get to meet soon," she said.

"Me too," I said.

"Can I call you again?"

"Absolutely."

"Don't by shy about calling me," she said.

We spoke on the phone twice more, but it was always a little awkward and stilted; we talked about the weather (a limited topic in

Southern California), what kind of clothes I liked, and what I hoped to do when I returned to San Francisco. Our conversations were still skimming over the surface of things. I'm not sure I could have expected much more.

A few weeks later, in July, Don called and said he was coming to San Diego, and asked whether I'd care to meet him and Jackie. I went to the airport to pick him up, and I remember being a little nervous. But then I realized that I was luckier than most people— after all, if I didn't like my brother, I didn't have to see him ever again. That thought quickly calmed me down.

I picked him out right away. He was tall, an inch or two over six feet, and handsome, with a thick mustache and furry eyebrows like mine (which are a bear to trim!). His eyes were as heavy-lidded and perfectly round as mine, but almost black in color; mine are dark brown, tinged with green.

"I'm Don," he said, and we shook hands.

"Anne," I said, smiling.

"Wow," he said. "You have a movie-star smile, just like Jackie. I didn't get that smile. That's why I grew a mustache."

We talked all the way from the airport to Point Loma, and I found it incredibly easy to be with him. He was kind, warm, personable, and clearly very concerned about my feelings. "If you change your mind about meeting Jackie, don't even think about it," he said. "I'll understand, and I know she'll understand."

I had arranged to have him spend the night at my parents' house, where I was living at the time, and they were waiting for us when we pulled in. They adored him. We gave Don time to freshen up, then piled into my dad's car and went to the Fish Market, a restaurant in downtown San Diego, for dinner. We all really liked Don. He was an intelligent, thoughtful man who had made his own way in the world, and he was about as well-adjusted and balanced a person as I'd ever met.

The next morning, a Saturday, we went off to meet Jackie. En route, Don recommended a couple of books on adoption—I think one of them was called *Lost and Found*—but I wasn't really all that curious. My life was good. I was worried that in reading accounts of how I was supposed to feel I'd open up a can of worms I didn't even know was there. Unlike Don, who had no family, I felt like the luckiest, most loved girl in the world.

"What do you call her?" I asked him.

"Jackie?" he asked. "I call her Mom. I've called her Mom since the day I met her."

I thought about this for a bit. I couldn't see myself calling her Mom. There was already a mom in my life, and she was pretty near perfect.

• • •

Jackie was living in Morro Bay at the time, four or five hours north, just past San Luis Obispo, but she had agreed to meet us in La Jolla, which was less than an hour away. Her son Scott, the golden boy, also lived in Morro Bay, with his girlfriend, Laci, and Don had met them on an earlier trip. "You won't get to meet them on this trip, but when you do, you'll fall in love with them both."

The rest of the kids were also grown, with lives of their own. There was John, who was Jackie's son by another man—although Lee Peterson had raised him as his own—and there were three kids from Lee's previous marriage: Mark, Susan, and Joe.

It was a beautiful day for a drive. As we neared La Jolla, Don told me that Jackie was not in good health. "Don't be shocked when you see her," he said. "She's on oxygen. She has a lung disease, but it's not emphysema, and it's not hereditary, and she was never a smoker. She was in an orphanage when she was little, and she had pneumonia so many times that it pretty much destroyed her lungs. No one's sure how long she's going to live."

We pulled up outside the Shell Beach Motel, which was right on the water. It was one of those older, Spanish-style places, with whitewashed walls and red tile roofs and flowers everywhere. We went inside and were directed to her room, and we made our way through the lobby and up a short flight of stairs. Don was watching me like a hawk.

"You okay?" he asked.

"Uh huh," I said. And I was. I felt fine. He was a very reassuring presence.

"Don't be nervous," he said. We stopped in front of her door, and he raised his hand to knock. "She's going to adore you."

"I'm not nervous—*really*," I said, laughing, although Don seemed so concerned that for a moment I wondered whether I had something to be nervous about. The moment passed, however. I wondered whether maybe I'd inherited a little bit of my adoptive father's personality: the way he's able to keep his feelings at bay.

Don knocked, and I heard approaching footfalls, and a moment later the door opened. Jackie Peterson, my birth mother, stood in the doorway and smiled. She was hooked up to a small oxygen tank, but it didn't make her less attractive, and she wasn't at all self-conscious about it.

"Come in, come in," she said, and she gave me a big, tentative hug. "It is so nice to meet you."

Don and I stepped through, and Jackie and I exchanged, brief appraising looks. *Now* I was a little nervous—more than a little, actually.

This is my mother, I was thinking. And she must have been thinking, *This is my daughter.*

"I was doing a little breathing treatment before you came in," she said, smiling. "I do that when I get stressed. I guess I was a little anxious about meeting you."

"It doesn't show," I said, and it really didn't.

Jackie showed us over to the couch; I took a seat, she sat on the other end, and Don pulled up a chair. "This is really a reunion for the two of you," he said. "I could leave and come back in an hour or two."

We both asked him to stay. He smiled, and I turned to look at Jackie.

"Do you like mushrooms?" she asked me.

"No," I said, although I was a bit thrown; I thought it was an odd question.

"What about colorful clothes?"

"No."

After a few more very specific questions—reading habits, sleep patterns, that kind of thing—it occurred to me that maybe she was just feeling around for signs that I was really her daughter, grasping for questions that might turn up a few genetic clues. She wanted to get a sense of some of the traits we shared, some of the things she had passed on.

Jackie seemed oddly comfortable in her shorts and her polo shirt—and, by the way, Uncle Al was right: She had lovely legs— and I think I was a little disappointed. I think I wanted her to be at least a little anxious, a little less matter-of-fact. After all, this was the woman who had given me up, and while I didn't expect an apology, I thought some kind of explanation would be nice. I asked her to describe the circumstances of my birth.

"You were conceived on a boat in the San Diego Bay," she said. "As soon as I found out I was pregnant, I went to a friend's house in Los Angeles and hid there for the duration. I lived off hot dogs. The only people in the world who knew I was pregnant were the woman

I was staying with and my brother Patrick. And Patrick is like a vault. He would never say anything to anyone."

For a moment I wondered why it was such a horrible, ugly secret. But thirty years ago, I knew, there was still more of a stigma attached to unwed motherhood than there is today.

"Your birth father found out about the pregnancy about a month before you were born, and he offered to marry me, but I wasn't interested," she went on. "Somehow, however, he found out what hospital I was in, and the day after you were born he showed up with some friends to visit."

I thought that was really strange, but she didn't think it was strange at all, and I didn't say anything.

She didn't have much to say about the day I was born—she didn't remember much about it, she said—then she went on to talk about her other sons, John and Scott, and her life with Lee. She kept going back to Scott, however. As Don had said, Scott was clearly her baby, her golden boy. And she actually used those words: *my golden boy*. As she talked about him, I noticed that her expression became soft and dreamy. "He was an incredible baby," she said, and suddenly she laughed, remembering something. "One night when he was still an infant, Lee and I took him to dinner with us, and we sat him in his little high chair. Throughout dinner, he was just as happy as can be, sitting there entertaining himself. He was so quiet, in fact, that we forgot he was there, and when we left the restaurant the waiter came running after us. 'Ma'am!' he said. 'You left your baby at the table!' I'll never forget that day."

There was much more to Jackie's life than that day at the restaurant, of course, and most of it was considerably darker. On December 23, 1945, when she was two years old, her father, John Latham, went missing. He owned a tire shop just outside San Diego. His wife, Helen, called the police in a panic, saying he hadn't come home. Officers found him the next day, Christmas Eve, under the Coronado Bridge, lying dead in a pool of blood, his skull cracked open, a metal pipe—the murder weapon—on the ground next to his body. They said it was a robbery gone wrong, and they eventually caught the man who did it, and he was tried, sentenced, and sent to prison for murder.

Unfortunately, Jackie's mother, Helen, fell completely apart in the wake of her husband's murder, and she was unable to care for her four children. Jackie ended up in an orphanage; she was reunited with her mother years later, but it was not a joyous reunion. Helen was sick, and Jackie was largely there in the role of caretaker.

"Those nuns never talked to me about sex," Jackie said with a sad smile. "I was very naive."

I didn't know what to say. I think this was Jackie's way of explaining why she had given birth to three kids out of wedlock, but I didn't want to pursue it, and she didn't say more.

"It's strange," she said, lost in thought. "Every time I went to tend to my mother, I'd open the door, and she'd say in that weak voice of hers, 'Is that you, Jacqueline?' And I'd always say, 'Yes, Mother, it's me.' And for years after she died, every time I opened a door, I would hear her voice again, 'Is that you, Jacqueline?' And I'd have to fight the urge to answer. Because she wasn't there. Because nobody was there."

• • •

"What did you think of her?" Don asked me after we'd said our good-byes and were en route back to Point Loma.

"I liked her," I said. "She sure didn't have an easy life."

Don stayed at my parents' one more night, and I drove him to the airport the next day and saw him off. Before the end of the week, he began writing me the sweetest letters. One of them began as follows:

Dear Anne,

Ever since I got home I haven't been able to stop thinking about our time together. Even though I had met our mother and siblings, I don't think I was prepared for how much you really mean to me. All of a sudden I feel very protective of you. Even though I know my other siblings, you are special to me like no other and NOBODY BETTER MESS WITH MY LITTLE SISTER! Ha!

It is also very comforting to know that if anything ever happens to our mother we will still have each other for a lifetime. . . .

I found it oddly comforting myself, although I didn't really feel much need to be comforted. I already had a great family. Don, however, had been through the wringer. He had lost both parents, he was estranged from his sister, and he was searching for connections. It seemed as if I should have been the one reaching out to him, comforting him, but he didn't need anything from me. He was just happy that we'd found each other and happy to be alive.

There were more letters from Don, and I wrote back, and it felt good. My world felt larger in the best possible sense. I also spoke to Jackie from time to time. She'd call, or I'd call, and there was an easy familiarity to our conversations. There was nothing deep about them, mind you. We would talk about cooking recipes or about the weather, but it was very pleasant, and I saw this as the beginning of a promising connection.

I had no idea what lay ahead.

At the Latham family reunion, 1998: Scott, Don, and Jackie

SCOTT

At the end of August, after three months of living at home, I moved back to San Francisco. I had always loved that city, and I felt I belonged there. Of course after three months at home I was eager to get out of my parents' hair and put my life in order. I had saved some money at Cubic, and an inexpensive apartment had just opened up in my old building, so I knew it was time to make my move.

When I told Jackie I was driving back to San Francisco, she begged me to stop in to see them in Morro Bay. "I want you to have dinner with us. I want you to meet Scott. You'll love him. You two are so alike."

Morro Bay is midway between San Diego and San Francisco. I made the drive, checked into a motel, and followed directions to Jackie's home. It was a beautiful little place on the water, and Lee Peterson hugged me the minute I walked through the door. He was a solid, warm man, and I took to him right away. Jackie gave me a hug and a kiss, and Lee got me a glass of wine and showed me around.

You could see the water from almost every room, and they had gorgeous furniture. Jackie owned an antique shop in Morro Bay; she was always wheeling and dealing, and the house was filled with armoires, ornate tables, and elegant lamps.

Lee was tall and tanned and a big fan of the Old West, and in fact he reminded me a little of a cowboy. One of the rooms in the house was decidedly his; with its Western motif, it actually looked like a movie set. There was an old wooden table with several hands of antique playing cards fanned out in front of each of the four chairs, along with an ancient whiskey bottle and four rusty shot glasses. Even the fixtures seemed to have come from the Old West, and the pièce de résistance was a full Civil War uniform Lee had put on display.

We sat down, and Jackie asked me about my plans in San Francisco, which were still nebulous. Then she told me that Scott was on his way over, very eager to meet his big sister. "I don't know if I told you," she said, "but he's engaged to be married."

"She's a nice girl," Lee piped up. "Name's Laci." I looked over at Lee, and it occurred to me that he seemed more cowboy-like than ever. Clearly, he was a man of few words.

Then Scott arrived. We could hear him pulling up outside, and we all stood up. I could see him through the screen door as he approached. It was eerie: Even at that distance, I recognized the features. We had the same round face and the same Latham eyes, and both of us had the Latham eyebrows—the ones Laci called "caterpillar brows." He walked in, already smiling, and it was a perfect smile. Right away I saw it. He really was the golden boy: handsome, athletic, and tall, with bright white teeth and nice skin and an actual glow about him. He could have been the poster boy for Southern California.

"You must be Scott," I said, and he laughed.

"You must be my big sister, Anne."

We shook hands and exchanged a few pleasantries—"nice to finally meet you," that kind of thing—and Jackie led us to the table. She had made pasta and a big salad, there was plenty of good wine, and I felt relaxed and comfortable with all of them, as if they'd been part of my family forever.

"Boy, you'd really like Laci," Scott said. "I can't wait for you to meet her."

He and Laci were living in San Luis Obispo, right above Morro

Bay. I think she was still studying horticulture, and I believe he had recently finished school.

"Look at them, Lee," Jackie said, changing the subject. "Look how similar they are. Isn't it uncanny?"

Lee just smiled and nodded, saying nothing, but Scott looked over at me and smiled that familiar smile—the smile I often saw on my own face, in pictures or in the mirror, the smile Don had described as a movie-star smile, just like Jackie's.

"I'm really glad I met you," Scott said. "This better not be a one-time thing. I want us to stay in touch, to be a family. I have plenty of brothers, but I'm kind of short on sisters."

He was a real charmer, the kind of guy who lights up a room. I had always considered myself a good judge of character, and I thought Scott was about as solid and genuine as they came. I kept thinking how interesting it was to have a family, and to lose them and to find them again, and to discover that they are really terrific people, your type of people. Many of these types of stories don't turn out this way. Some people who connect with their biological parents find the results disappointing, if not downright heartbreaking, but this was definitely not the case here. If I'd been worried about unpleasant surprises, my worries were over. These were decent, loving people, with good, solid values.

The wine helped, too, of course; it's amazing how pleasant the world can seem after a glass or two. That was another thing Scott and I shared: our love of wine. I told him I liked chardonnays, zinfandels, and pinot noirs, and—in the Napa Valley—I was partial to the Napa, Sonoma, and Russian River wines. Scott was knowledgeable, but he said he was still learning. "I just like wine," he said.

When the coffee came, Lee told a story about a recent fishing trip with Scott, and how the boat kept getting pulled out by the tide, and both of them had to fight like hell to get back to shore. "We're laughing about it now," Scott said, "but we weren't laughing then."

I really liked these people, and I especially liked Scott. I kept staring at those familiar features. It was a little trippy, actually. But I liked it. I had a brother who looked like me. This guy was family to the bone.

. . .

The next morning, Jackie took me into town to see her mechanic. My car was heating up, and she didn't want me to make the rest of the drive without having someone take a look, which sounded like a good idea. So I followed her into Morro Bay, where we dropped off the car, and then she took me to see her antique shop. I bought a little beaded embroidery that dated back to eighteenth-century France, and she gave me a nice discount—although I admit it felt a little strange, doing business with my mother.

As she was making change, a friend of hers came into the store.

"This is my daughter," Jackie said, and that didn't sit well with me. I shook hands with her friend, and I was polite, but after the woman left I turned to Jackie and told her that the situation had felt a little weird.

"I know," she said. "I'm sorry. It felt a little weird to me, too."

"I didn't mean it as a criticism. . . ."

"No, no," she said. "I understand. I overstepped my bounds. It's just that I'm so proud of you, and I'm so happy to have you back in my life."

Later, as we went back to the mechanic's place to get my car, I thought about why this had bothered me so much, and it seemed pretty obvious: I already had a mother. Jackie hadn't earned the right to be called Mom, not by me, anyway, and I wasn't sure she ever would. For Don, who had lost both his parents, it was different. He was thrilled to have somebody he could call Mom. "It was effortless," he had told me. "It felt right."

But it didn't feel right to me. And then I remembered that Stephen had experienced similar difficulties with his own birth mother, who had made contact with him several years earlier. He couldn't call her Mom, either. He was nice to her, but he was firm: "I only have one mom," he said, and she had understood. It hurt, I'm sure, but she got the point.

"How about if I call you my fairy godmother?" I suggested. My car was fixed and ready to go, and there'd been no charge.

"Fairy godmother is perfect," Jackie said. "You'll be my fairy goddaughter."

We hugged and said good-bye, and I got in my car and went on my way. I could see Jackie in the rearview mirror, waving from a distance; then I made a right at the corner, and she was gone.

• • •

I moved back into my old building, into a smaller, less expensive apartment, and began looking around for a job. I kept running into Tim Bird, my old suitor, who lived in the old neighborhood, and from time to time we got together for a drink. Still, I wasn't sure what he had in mind, and—thanks to that unhappy, short-lived marriage—I remained very cautious around men.

Meanwhile, with my blessing, my mother and Jackie were making plans to meet. They decided on a little restaurant in Fallbrook, just north of San Diego, and went out for lunch.

They both reported back that same afternoon. Jackie said my mother couldn't have been nicer, and she was actually somewhat surprised by how similar they were. Both women are petite, with dark hair and bangs. "She said she felt blessed to have such a wonderful daughter," Jackie told me. "And *I'm* relieved, too. I'm happy you were raised by such a wonderful woman."

I felt blessed, too, but I didn't think it was necessary to share that feeling with Jackie. I'm sure this was all fairly trying for her, emotionally, and she was being incredibly gracious. I could be gracious, too.

Then my mother called to tell me that she'd found Jackie very charming. She thought it was nice that Don, Jackie, Lee, and Scott had turned out to be such wonderful people, and she was genuinely happy for me. "This has been the best possible outcome," she said. "You couldn't have done better. To find people like that anywhere in the world, and to find them because they're family—well, that's a real gift."

I went home for Christmas and then returned and went to work for RobertsonStevens, an investment bank in San Francisco. Don kept writing me nice letters, and I still talked to Jackie from time to time, but everyone seemed unusually busy, especially Scott and Laci, who were getting married.

That February, right about the time I heard their good news, romance entered my own life. Two days before Valentine's Day, Tim called and left a message, wondering if I had a date for the big night. My sister, Susan, was visiting from San Diego, and she thought he sounded nice. She urged me to return his call. "I don't know what your problem is," she said. "He sounds great."

I took her advice and took Tim up on his invitation for Valentine's Day. I'd been out with him before, of course, but the other times had been more casual—a drink at the neighborhood bar, a slice of pizza. This was a *date* date, in every sense of the word.

He took me to a very chic restaurant that didn't even have a sign out front. You either knew the place or you didn't, and if you stumbled across it by accident and weren't a regular you probably wouldn't get in. It was very romantic, and the food was wonderful—I remember the carpaccio and the buttery escargots—and I also remember that we drank a little too much wine.

Tim walked me home; he didn't get lucky that night, but I had a feeling he might get lucky in the near future. He was a very nice guy and incredibly easy to talk to. He called me the next day and asked me out again, and we began to date in earnest, slowly getting to know each other. Tim was born just outside town, in Redwood City; he'd grown up to be an electrical contractor, and now he was working on large-scale projects in and around San Francisco.

Before long I'd met Tim's sister and his parents, too. Both sets. They were divorced and had long since settled into new lives. His father was living in San Carlos, near Redwood City, and his mother and her new husband shuttled between San Francisco and Wyoming. They were wonderful people. I know I said the same thing about the Lathams; by now it must sound as if I like everyone indiscriminately. But that's not the case at all. I actually think of myself as a discerning, cautious person, and I don't rush into friendships easily. At the time, I just thought I'd hit a lucky patch. Maybe it was fate; I don't know. All I know is that good people kept coming into my life.

· · ·

Early that summer, Jackie called to tell me about Scott and Laci's upcoming wedding. She said she had wanted to invite me, but that Laci didn't seem all that comfortable with the idea, never having met me. I told her I totally agreed. I wouldn't have been comfortable either, especially since I would have found myself in a room with dozens of new relatives, *relative strangers*, as it were, and I didn't think I was prepared, psychologically, for something of that magnitude. Scott later called to make sure I understood, and I reiterated what I told Jackie. "I couldn't go even if you invited me," I said. "Please. We'll meet later in the year."

"Thanks for being so understanding," Scott said, ever the gentleman. "I'm going to make sure you and Laci meet as soon as possible. You guys are going to love each other."

*   *   *

Scott and Laci were married on August 9, 1997, at the Sycamore Mineral Springs Resort, near San Luis Obispo.

A month later, I got a call from Jackie. She said she and Lee were going to spend a few days in Carmel, a lovely town by the sea, and Scott and Laci were going to be joining them. "I want to see you, and Scott wants to see you, and Laci desperately wants to meet you," she said. "Please say yes."

I drove down to Carmel the following weekend. Jackie had booked a room for me at Svendsgaard's Inn, a cute little bed-and-breakfast with a country theme and piney furniture, where they were all staying. I checked in, dropped off my bag in my room, and called Jackie to let her know I'd arrived, and a moment later I went down to the courtyard to meet Laci. She and Jackie were waiting for me. Jackie introduced us, and I couldn't get over how pretty she was. She reminded me of a Madame Alexander doll: the porcelain-like skin, the dark eyes with those thick, perfect lashes, and that huge, dimpled smile.

Laci seemed very wired and very happy to meet me. Jackie and Scott had both gone on and on about me, she said.

"Where is Scott?" I asked.

"He and Lee are in town," Jackie said. "Doing boy stuff. Who knows?"

Jackie, Laci, and I strolled into town as well, and Laci just talked and talked, tirelessly. She kept telling me how exciting it was to have a sister-in-law, especially one who came so highly recommended. At first I thought she was going a little overboard, but slowly I came to see that this was just Laci: full of love, warmth, energy, and enthusiasm for life and for people.

"Do you know what Scott told me when he came home after

that first night he met you?" she asked. "He said that when he looked into your face it was like looking into a mirror. He just couldn't get over it. He has two other siblings, Don, who lives back east, and John, but he said he looks most like you, and that he felt most connected to you."

"That's weird," I said. "I thought it was kind of trippy, too. When he walked in the door at Jackie's house, I was stunned by how much alike we were."

"We're going to be great girlfriends," Laci said.

By this time Jackie had led the way inside Pierre Deux, a French country store in Carmel that happens to be one of her favorite stores in the world. Pierre Deux is full of teapots and wall plates and dinnerware, and those Quimper figurines; it's really not my cup of tea. But Jackie was emoting over everything she saw. I didn't say a word—my family is old school: If you don't have something nice to say, say nothing—but I looked over at Laci and she rolled her big eyes at me. Clearly, this wasn't her style either.

I did, however, see a plate I liked, and Laci crept up behind me. "So," she joked. "I see you've inherited Jackie's French country gene."

"Maybe a little," I said. "But within reason."

I thought it was funny how Laci was so quick to look for similarities between Jackie and me, as if she wanted to imagine us as mother and daughter. Then again, she had never met my family, so it would have been difficult for her to remember that my real mother was a woman who lived back in Point Loma.

• • •

That night we all went to a fancy little restaurant together. Scott and Laci sat next to each other, so close together that their shoulders were touching. They were holding hands and smiling at each other and eating off each other's plates, and they looked like the happiest newlyweds in the world. Scott was beaming—at her, at us, at the world at large.

Laci was a big talker, but not in a bad, chatty-Kathy way. She was just bubbling over with energy. She asked me about San Francisco, about the kind of job I was looking for, and whether I was dating.

"Well, I'm dating," I admitted. "There's this guy, Tim. It looks like it's getting pretty serious."

After dinner, we walked back to the hotel and made it an early night, and in the morning I woke up and found a beautiful little breakfast basket outside my door. It was filled with muffins and fruit and fresh juice, and later I told Jackie how beautifully it had been arranged, and that it had been a very pleasant way to start the day.

"You should have seen Laci's basket," she said, and she made a little face. "Laci always has to redo everything. She's a perfectionist. You give her something that's already perfect, but she'll still find a way to improve it."

It wasn't exactly a compliment. Jackie seemed to be hinting that Laci took Martha Stewart a little more seriously than nature intended. I'd later learn she was right, but in truth I kind of loved that side of Laci. It was endearing to meet someone who had so much flair for that type of thing, and who seemed determined to make the world a prettier, more appealing place.

We walked along Pebble Beach later that morning, past the golf course and across the beautifully landscaped grounds. In the distance I could see the waves crashing against the rocks: another perfect, California day.

When we passed the golf shop, I saw a pair of $400 golf shoes and found myself thinking maybe I should take up golf and that those shoes would probably really help my game. Then I heard a voice behind me. "Look at these incredible pansies!" It was Laci. She had her back to the store window, and she was staring at the oak-barrel planters, which were ablaze with color. She was far more interested in flowers than in golf shoes. "Aren't these the most beautiful pansies you've ever seen?"

I wasn't sure; I'd never given much thought to pansies. I was a city mouse, and it looked like Laci was shaping up to be my country cousin. But I took a look at those pansies, and they really were quite beautiful. And in the months ahead, under Laci's influence, I fell in love with flowers, too.

. . .

We caught up with the others and went off to lunch, and I couldn't get over how polite Scott was. He was a perfect gentleman, almost old-fashioned, in fact. He got the door for me. He pulled out my chair. He made sure everyone had a menu before he reached for his own. He even deferred to me on the choice of wine.

In retrospect, it all seems a little bit unreal. It may be that my assessment is colored by the horror that came later; I'm not sure. It just seemed a little too studied, a little too perfect. Even when Scott addressed me, he looked right into my eyes, almost as if he knew that it was what you were supposed to do, not realizing that it was perhaps a little too intense.

"Hey, Sis, what are you going to have for lunch?"

Scott called me Sis right away, and I didn't mind it at all. Somehow it felt right with him. He was very happy to have a sister, and I accepted it. And anyway, unlike motherhood, being a sibling isn't something you have to earn.

At the time, I was totally charmed by Scott. I liked the eye contact, intense as it might have been, and I liked the way he gave me his undivided attention, as if he were wholly absorbed in everything I was saying, no matter how trivial or unimportant. I wondered if he'd learned to be a good listener from being with Laci, who was such a good talker. I don't know. All I know is that I found myself thinking that they were both very lucky: Laci because Scott was such a classy, cultured, caring man and Scott because Laci was so warm, so full of life, and such a kick in the pants. The golden boy and his doll-like bride: What could be better?

After lunch we went for another stroll through town, on our way back to the hotel, and I found myself bringing up the rear with Jackie. I remarked on how happy she must be with Laci, and how happy Scott seemed with his new wife. She shrugged and made a little face. She didn't say anything bad about Laci, but she told me she couldn't stand Modesto, and she was worried that Laci was going to talk Scott into moving there. "It's a nothing little town on the wrong side of the tracks," she said. "I don't like it at all."

I'd been through Modesto a number of times, and it had always seemed pleasant enough to me. I wondered if there was more to what Jackie was saying, but I didn't question her.

I looked up the street. Laci had her nose buried in another planter. She seemed to know the name of every flower on the planet. She was deeply interested in horticulture, and she was going to try to make a career of it.

"I want to get into ornamental horticulture," she told me. This was something I had never heard of and didn't even know existed. "I love flowers. I like plants, too, but there's nothing like flowers. Anything that blooms, I'm interested."

We got back to the hotel, checked out, and said our good-byes in the parking lot. Scott carried my bag, put it into the trunk of my car, and got my door for me.

I gave Laci a big hug good-bye and gave more tempered hugs to Jackie, Scott, and Lee. I remember standing there studying these three people, people I was just getting to know, and thinking about the little curves life throws at you, and how pleasant some of them turn out to be.

"Hey, Sis, nice seeing you again," Scott said. "Don't be a stranger."

"Call me," Laci said.

"I will," I said, and I got into my car and drove away.

I hadn't been back a week—still working at the bank and still happily dating Tim—when I received a letter from Don. "It sounds like you guys had fun in Carmel," he wrote. "Jackie is a lot of fun to be with and so are you. The two of you must have had a great time together." He closed with, "I think of you a lot and miss you very much. . . . Love, your brother . . . Don."

I spent Christmas in San Diego, with the Grady Bunch, and early in 1998 I went back to Carmel with the Petersons for two more visits. It was always more of the same—carefree strolls through town, family gossip at lunch, a little shopping, and enjoyably drawn out dinners over good cabernets and better pinot noirs. At the end of the night Jackie and Lee always went back to their room, and I would hang out with Scott and Laci: just the three of us.

I loved being with them. I loved the way they loved each other. I loved the fact that my new, second family was beginning to feel like an extension of my real family, of the people I had known and loved my whole life.

• • •

In late 1998 the Lathams had a family reunion, and Jackie called and invited me to go along. It was going to be held at the Shell Beach Motel, where I had first met Jackie; I thanked her for inviting me and told her I'd be delighted to go.

I took Tim, and we drove to San Diego, where I introduced him to my parents. They were wild about him, which made me happy. I think I wanted their approval before I let myself get too hopeful, but now I was genuinely hopeful.

The Latham reunion turned out to be a real hoot. It was mostly people from Jackie's side of the family, and it was a very colorful collection (to put it mildly). Most of them had those wild "caterpillar brows," and they were very gossipy.

"See that cousin there? He's the gay one. And that's the family lesbian. But that's about it in that department." I was the latest addition to the family, another member of the extended clan to share all the details with—including the dirt. I loved it.

Scott and Laci were there, too, and they met Tim. "This is the golden boy," I said, joking around. But I noticed that Scott didn't find it amusing. He seemed to take the title quite seriously, and I made a mental note to stop making light of it.

Later that day, I remember walking through the motel grounds with Jackie, and I saw a trail of roses leading down a path toward one of the cottage-like rooms. "Isn't that cute?" I asked.

Jackie rolled her eyes. "That's Laci," she said. "That's her and Scott's room. Only Laci would take the time to do something like that."

"I think it's really nice," I said.

Jackie shrugged. "Well, maybe you're right. They *are* newlyweds."

By the end of the visit, Tim had bonded with Jackie's older brother John. He owned a lodge in Alaska, and he was a big game hunter. He loved all the same things Tim loved: hunting, fishing, wildlife, nature, and canoeing. John is a real rugged, outdoorsy type, but the moment you meet him you get a sense of a good man with a strong, moral center. I liked him, too. He seemed to be very solid: the unofficial leader of the clan.

John took the time to tell me a little bit about their early years. All the children ended up in different homes, he said, and poor Jackie got stuck in a terrible orphanage. But they managed to stay close, and that's what the reunions were all about. Staying in touch. Remembering who you were and where you came from.

People kept coming up to me and telling me what a great guy Tim was. And Scott kept nudging me and asking if this was the one, if we were going to get married.

"Give us a little time," I said, laughing. "It's funny how married people always want everyone else to hurry up and get married. What's the rush?"

"You'll soon find out," Scott said.

The next day we were preparing for a huge family lunch, setting up outdoors on two big, wooden tables that had been pushed together. I had brought linens and plates and things, and I was setting the table, and when Laci came out she was very impressed by the fact that I knew where the knives went and which way the blade was supposed to be pointing.

"That's really good," she said.

"Thanks," I said.

I was amused. With Laci, it wasn't about being snobby. It was about doing things properly. She loved detail. She would have made Martha Stewart proud, imposing order and beauty on everything she touched.

That night, the last night, Tim and I went to a Mexican restaurant in town with Laci, Scott, Jackie, and Lee. We had too many margaritas and too much rich food, and I looked around and thought how lucky I was to have these people in my life.

"That Laci sure talks a lot," Tim whispered in my ear.

She did talk a lot. But that was one of her endearing qualities. Some people talk when they're nervous. Laci talked because she was happy. And she was always happy.

Or so the rest of us thought.

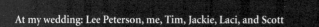
At my wedding: Lee Peterson, me, Tim, Jackie, Laci, and Scott

FAMILY

S hortly after we got back to San Francisco, I found out about a great job at Montgomery Securities, another investment bank. This was during the tail end of the dot-com mergers, before the writing was on the wall, and I got the job and hit the ground running. The company was handling some major mergers and acquisitions, and everyone was working at breakneck speed.

A few weeks later, just as I was beginning to enjoy the mad pace at work, Tim asked me to marry him. I'd like to say it was fueled by all the good times and all the family togetherness, but the fact is that I was pregnant. Don't get me wrong: I knew Tim was the man for me. But I'm a traditional, old-fashioned girl, and I wish things hadn't been so rushed. In the space of a frenetic month, I planned both my wedding and the reception.

We had a big party at Plumpjack, one of the great San Francisco restaurants, and our families meshed beautifully. Similar sensibilities, similar senses of humor, similar values—and of course a great love of wine.

The wedding took place on August 28, 1999, and the invitation read as follows:

Mr. and Mrs. Thomas Bell Grady
request the honor of your presence
at the marriage of their daughter
Anne Elizabeth
to
Mr. Timothy James Bird
Saturday, the twenty-eighth of August
Nineteen hundred and ninety-nine
at ten o'clock in the morning
Grace Cathedral
San Francisco

The reception was at the Top of the Mark, another fancy restaurant—this one in the Mark Hopkins Hotel. The Petersons were well represented. Jackie and Lee were there, as were Scott and Laci. Scott was wearing a peach-colored shirt that matched Laci's dress. It was clearly her doing, and it worked beautifully. For her part, Jackie arrived in a light blue outfit that matched the outfits on my bridesmaids, although I don't think this was deliberate.

With four sets of families there—Tim's divorced parents and their respective mates, along with my parents and Jackie and Lee—I was a little worried about the chemistry. But the event was a huge success.

Laci went out of her way to tell me that she had loved *almost* every detail of the wedding, which made me laugh. I don't think the flowers were up to her high standards.

"I just want you to know I love having you in my life," she said. "And I'm jealous that you're pregnant."

Ryan Bird was born in February, a scant five months after the wedding (just in case you're doing the math), in our new home, a brick house in Berkeley overlooking the San Francisco Bay. He was a little ball of fire, and he looked exactly like Tim, who decided to call him Mini Me; almost five years later, he still does.

I took three months of maternity leave, and while I was away there was a big shake up and Montgomery Securities was purchased by Nations Bank, and then in turn by BancAmerica Securities. Somehow, however, I managed to survive both purges and stayed until the following May. During those last weeks I was involved in various mergers, and I received a handsome bonus when I left.

The next thing I knew, I was pregnant again. After telling my family, I called Jackie to share the good news. Laci got pregnant just a short time later, and Jackie called to let me know. When I called Laci, she was bubbling over, ecstatic.

"I can't wait!" she said.

Laci and Scott had finally moved to Modesto after all, and Scott was working for Tradecorp, a fertilizer company. They had bought a nice home with a swimming pool, and Laci was very happy to be pregnant. She was also delighted to be living near her mother, Sharon Rocha, and her stepfather, Ron Grantski.

Now that we'd reconnected, we stayed in touch. Laci came to me for child-rearing tips, since I already had plenty of experience with Ryan, and I came to her for tips on gardening. By now I'd caught Laci's love of flowers in a big way; I had turned our entire yard into an all-blue garden, with heavy emphasis on blue pansies. I then took a can of blue paint and went to work on the front gate, the front door, and the children's playhouse. Maybe I got a little carried away, but I loved it.

I also spoke to Jackie from time to time. During one of those calls, she told me that Laci had been complaining about maternity clothes, which she found horrendously overpriced.

"That's how they get you," I said. "You're so hormonal that you don't know what you're doing, and you whip out your credit card."

After I got off the phone, I went to look for some of my old maternity clothes and packed up a few of the nicer outfits and sent them to Laci in Modesto. She was still in her first trimester, and I knew she'd fit into them, although I wasn't sure they'd be up to her usual high standards.

"I can't believe this!" Laci said. She was calling to thank me for the clothes. "That was so nice of you!"

"Did you like them?"

"Yes," she said. "Most of them."

I laughed. That was another thing I loved about Laci. She was incredibly honest.

Jackie was another story. She wasn't quite as straightforward as her daughter-in-law. She would call from time to time to make sure I was up on the family news. "They're not going to be there forever," she said, sounding less than happy. "They're on the five-year plan."

"Meaning what?"

"Meaning they're not going to be staying in that town for the rest of their lives."

I didn't ask why she disliked Modesto because I thought I knew. There was the reason she'd already told me: She thought it was on the wrong side of the tracks. And there was the reason I sensed on my own: Her golden boy was too far from home.

"That was nice of you to send those clothes to Laci," she said. "I wonder if she'll wear any of them."

I didn't pursue that line of thinking. I was beginning to understand why Jackie was so critical of Laci. No one was good enough for her golden boy.

What I didn't understand was why Jackie was so dismissive of Laci's almost obsessive attention to detail. I thought it was endearing, the way she wanted to leave her mark on everything, and I imagined Scott enjoyed it, too. Whenever I talked to Laci, she was incredibly upbeat, especially lately, with the pregnancy. She seemed thrilled to be living in Modesto, with Scott, with their life together. She seemed especially thrilled about the baby.

I sent her a bunch of baby clothes, too, making sure to include only the nicest outfits, the ones she might actually use, and she called to thank me the minute they arrived. She also told me that she wanted me to meet her family. "You'll love my mom," she noted.

In July, when I was already more than eight months pregnant, my brother Don sent his eighteen-year-old daughter and a friend to visit. It was nice to see her again—I hadn't seen her since my wedding, when we first met—but in my condition it was hard to keep up with two teenagers. Both girls had just graduated from high school, and they were in party mode, and I was fifty pounds past my ideal weight, waddling, and my entire body hurt. I had to wear clogs because I couldn't bend over to tie my shoes.

One afternoon I dropped onto the couch, exhausted, and called Laci to see if she would take the two girls off my hands for a night or two.

"I wish I could," Laci said. "I'm too pregnant myself."

"Really?" I asked. "Wait till you're my size."

But there was something in what she'd said that concerned me. For one thing, she was barely in her second trimester; she shouldn't be feeling "too pregnant," not yet. For another, she wasn't as bubbly and talkative as usual.

"Everything okay?" I asked.

"Yeah," she said. "Great."

The conversation petered out, and I went to tend to Ryan and my houseguests.

At the end of the week, my niece and her friend went off to visit grandma Jackie. I had an old sapphire ring I didn't want anymore, nothing too fancy, more of a cocktail ring, really, and I asked my niece to give it to Jackie. "Tell her she can try to sell it at her antique shop," I said. I figured Jackie would take care of me if she ever managed to get rid of it, and I left it at that.

Jackie called after the two girls had gone back east.

"How are you?" she asked.

"Good," I said. "Ready to explode. How were the girls? Did they have a nice time?"

"Yes," Jackie said. "Have you talked to Laci lately?"

"A few days ago," I said.

"Did Laci say anything?" she asked. "I think they're having problems."

"Not a word," I said. But I thought back to the last time we talked and how different she had sounded. "Do you know what's wrong?"

"No. No idea. Those two, I can't figure them out."

Then she said she had to go—she had some paperwork to do—and hung up. It was almost as if she was throwing her hands up in despair.

I was worried, but not overly so. If there was one thing about Laci that gave me hope, it was her faith in the potential for perfection. Everything in her life had to be just right. If she was having problems with Scott, I knew she would do everything in her power to fix it.

· · ·

When my son Tommy was born in late August 2002, my first thought was, *We have to go to Disneyland.* I know it may sound crazy, going off to Disneyland with a two-year-old and an infant, and I'd like to tell you that I was just being a great mother, thinking of the kids. But the truth is, Tim and I really like Disneyland. Some people might say we even have a little problem with Disneyland. But so what? We all have our demons.

The first person I called was Jackie. "How would you and Lee like to get all the kids together and go to Disneyland in November?"

"You just had a baby!"

"Nothing like walking around the Magic Kingdom to get back into shape," I said.

Jackie didn't think Lee would go, but she was game. She said she knew that Scott's brother John and his wife, Alison, would want to go, and she would try to talk Scott and Laci into going on the trip.

"I thought they loved Disneyland," I said.

"Yeah, well, they're having problems again."

"Again?" I asked. "What kind of problems?"

"I don't know," Jackie said, sighing. "Just—you know—men."

"What do you mean?"

"It's nothing," Jackie said. "Laci's tired all the time—with the pregnancy and everything. Forget I said anything."

I could see she wanted to drop it, so I dropped it. I called John and Alison, and she called Scott, and when we connected later it looked like everyone was on board—everyone except Lee. "Disneyland is not his idea of a good time," Jackie said.

"But Laci and Scott are coming?" I asked.

"Probably," Jackie said. "They're working on it."

When I got off the phone, I couldn't stop thinking about Scott and Laci. What did she mean, *men*? That was so unlike Jackie. She only ever had nice things to say about her golden boy. What could be going on? I couldn't begin to imagine it. You always heard stories about guys freaking out when their wives got pregnant and running off or having affairs. But Scott didn't seem like the type. And most men got over it, right?

Whatever it was, I was sure they'd handle it.

• • •

In November, we all met at Disneyland. Tim and I and the two boys arrived a day ahead of everyone else, but the trip got off to an unpromising start. We were on the monorail, on our way to the hotel, and it was a hot, windy night. The windows on the monorail were open, and Ryan dropped something, and Tim bent down to pick it up. At that very instant, a huge branch flew through the window and whipped across the top of Tim's seat. Tim sat up.

"What was that?" he asked.

I couldn't answer. I felt as if I was watching a movie, but I didn't know whether it was a comedy or a thriller. All I knew is that Tim had come very close to getting decapitated.

The next thing that happened was at one of the restaurants. We were having breakfast the following morning, and Tommy was in his car seat, and Brer Bear accidentally bumped into Tommy, who fell and hit his head against the table and began to cry.

It felt like half the staff came running over to help us, including Brer Bear, and we eventually got everything under control. Poor Brer Bear kept apologizing, and I had to keep reassuring him that everything was all right, until finally the big stuffed animal went on his way.

The next morning, per our arrangement, we met everyone else at the winery inside Disney's California Adventure. They had already checked into their rooms, and most of them weren't happy. We were all booked into the same hotel, but we seemed to be at opposite ends of the place, and no amount of shuffling was going to change that. Jackie was especially unhappy because she was on oxygen and the hotel was so big that just making it to the end of her hallway seemed like an accomplishment. Laci had a similar problem. She was feeling very large and very tired, and Scott had rented a wheelchair for her, more or less as a joke. I kept looking at them, searching for some sign of trouble, trying to figure out what Jackie had meant—"They're having problems again"—but I didn't notice anything.

"How are you holding up?" I asked Jackie. I noticed she was fiddling with her oxygen tank.

"Okay, I guess. I'm with two pregnant women and one woman who just gave birth, so I'll feel badly if I can't keep up."

I felt awful. The only people who seemed calm and happy were John and Alison. For a while there, I thought the entire trip—which had been my idea to begin with—was going to turn into a complete fiasco. But we went off to the park and began to enjoy ourselves, and by the time we met for dinner that night, at the Napa Rose, a fancy restaurant inside the Grand California Hotel, everyone seemed to be relaxing.

I had made the dinner reservations, and I had asked for a nice table, and the staff came through for us. We had the nicest table in the house, and Laci had the best seat at the table, with a great view through the tall, ornate glass windows of the roaring fire pit outside. Laci looked amazing. She was wearing a baby doll–style dress over her big belly, and she was full of energy. I have never seen a more excited pregnant woman in my life.

"I can't wait to have this baby," she said.

"I know," I said. "The last month or two is sheer torture."

"No, not that," she said. "I'm just excited."

She asked if she could borrow Tommy, and I handed him over. She bounced him up and down and cooed at him. "How'm I doing?" she asked.

"Great," I said, laughing.

"Tell me the truth," she said. "I don't have much time left to practice."

"You're a natural," I said, amused.

When the menus arrived, I took Tommy and put him in his car seat, and Scott helped me strap him in. He then took the car seat and set it next to him and began to play with Tommy's tiny hands.

"Are you excited?" I asked, referring to the coming child.

"Oh yeah," he said. "I can't wait to play football with the little guy."

An innocent-sounding comment, I know. But there was something odd about the way he said it. It just seemed *flat* to me. It almost felt as if he were saying it only because he knew it was the right thing to say; his words seemed completely devoid of emotion. For a moment I wondered if I was looking for some signs of trouble, given what Jackie had told me, but I didn't think so. There was something different about Scott that night. He was there, and he looked as handsome as ever, and he smiled at all the appropriate times. But there was also something distant about him. There were moments when I felt he wasn't really there at all.

Then it got stranger. Scott ordered a very nice bottle of wine with dinner, and he never once passed it. He just parked it next to his plate and kept it there all night. Seeing that he wasn't going to get any of that fine wine, Tim ordered a glass for himself and one for me.

I turned my attention to Laci. "I'm so glad you're having a boy," I said.

"Me too," said Laci. "What do you think of the name 'Logan?'"

"I love it."

"I don't." It was Jackie, piping up from her end of the table. "I don't like it at all."

She said it in a very mean way, and when I looked over at Laci I was surprised by how distressed she looked. It was as if someone had slapped her across the face. This was a girl who was always happy, always smiling; I'd never seen her smile disappear that way before.

"You'll figure it out," I said.

And just like that, Laci smiled again: that big old smile. In an instant, she had willed herself to snap out of it. I wondered if the problems Jackie had alluded to were between her and Laci, not between Laci and Scott. And when the food began to arrive, I became more convinced that this was indeed the case. Scott and Laci had split one of those extravagant, six-course, prix fixe dinners, and they compared notes after every bite. The glazed pear salad with walnuts and blue cheese. The cold asparagus. The vegetable terrine. They would take a bite and close their eyes and chew slowly, savoring each morsel, and then turn toward each other and compare notes.

"Unbelievable."

"That melted in my mouth."

"Did you taste the spices in that?"

Scott was back to his old self. I looked over at his bottle of wine. He had practically polished it off, which may have had something to do with the sudden change in mood. I looked over at Tim. He was busy flagging the waiter for another glass of the cheap stuff.

In the lull before dessert arrived, Laci looked over at me and smiled that big, dimply smile of hers. "My back's killing me," she said. That was Laci: Even when she was complaining about her aching back, she was smiling to beat the band.

"I know what you mean," I said. "With both boys, my last month was pretty much nonstop whining and moaning."

"You know what I do?" she said. "I climb into the pool whenever it gets bad. That takes all the weight off my back, and it feels great, just sort of floating there by the edge. No gravity."

I never thought to ask whether the pool was heated. It was November, and this side of the country usually doesn't get cold till late in the year. Still, there's nothing worse than a cold pool in winter.

When dessert arrived, Laci pushed hers toward Scott. "My doctor said I shouldn't gain more than thirty-five pounds total," she said, explaining it to me. "I'm trying to be careful."

"Thirty-five pounds?!" I shot back. "I gained *sixty*!" Suddenly *I* felt like Brer Bear.

After dinner, Laci and I went to the ladies' room, and I was still full of sisterly advice. "There's something you should do before the baby comes along," I said. "When I had Ryan, my mother could only stay for a few weeks, and it was really hard without help. So you should try to arrange to get help as soon as you get back to Modesto, before the baby comes. Because after the baby, it'll be too crazy."

"No," she said. "I don't need help. My mother is going to be there every day."

I thought this was either naive or wishful thinking, and I thought I ought to tell her so. "That's what people say," I told her. "Then they come over a couple of times, and you never hear from them again."

"Not my mother," she said. "My mother can't wait for this baby. She's as excited as I am. We'll be fighting over who gets to hold him. You don't know my mother. She will be there every day." Laci was adamant on this point.

I reached into my purse for my lipstick and started putting it on.

"What kind of lipstick is that?" she asked.

"I don't know," I said. "It's called 'plumping' lipstick. It's supposed to plump up your lips."

"Does it work?" she asked.

"I don't know. Look at my lips. Do they look plumper?"

She looked dubious. "How much did you pay for that lipstick?" she asked.

"Thirty bucks," I said.

"Then it definitely works!" she said, and we both laughed.

When we got back to the table, Ryan was standing by Laci's chair. He had started calling her Aunt Laci that morning because I'd been referring to her as Aunt Laci, and now I took one of his hands and put it on her belly. "That's your little cousin in there," I said. Then I lowered my voice so Jackie wouldn't hear. "We're not sure about his name yet, but we still have time to decide. And whatever it is, you'll get to play with him."

The bill came and everyone chipped in—some of us paying a

little more than we might have, to subsidize Scott's wine—and we all returned to the hotel. Laci and I ended up walking together, and I felt a little bad because I wasn't spending any time with either John or Alison. But I couldn't help myself. By this time, Laci and I had pretty much become sisters.

"Is it scary, giving birth?" she asked me.

"A little bit. At the very end. But then you realize that millions of women have already gone through it, and you know you'll survive."

"I'm not looking forward to the pain," she said.

"I wouldn't know about the pain," I said. "I had C-sections with both of them."

"Really?"

I nodded. "There's nothing wrong with C-sections, you know. I actually think it's a lot less traumatizing, for both the mother and the baby. And there's a plus side: They pop out looking perfect."

· · ·

The next morning, Tim and I were up at six because both boys were raring to go. At that point, as any parent knows, you're in it for the long haul, so we pulled ourselves together, had a slow, leisurely breakfast, and made our way into the park. We were scheduled to meet the others at noon, and we did, but by that time Tim and I were so beat that we begged off. We went back to the hotel to see if we could put the boys down for a nap, hoping we could take a nap, too.

But Tim got a second wind and took off, saying he'd be back within the hour. Before long both boys were fast asleep, and I went over to the bed and stretched out. The moment my head touched the pillow, however, the fire alarm went off. I *freaked*. I had to carry the two boys down four flights of stairs, alone, and the lobby was crowded with grumbling people. One of the grumbling people was

Jackie, who had also gone back to the room to rest—only to turn around and make her way down all those flights of stairs, carrying her oxygen supply. Needless to say, she wasn't happy.

The afternoon was a bust. We just didn't have the energy for anything else, and we ended up congregating in Jackie's suite, where we exchanged Christmas presents. We had to walk down several endless corridors to get there, and I made a mental note to myself to look for a smaller hotel the next time I planned a family vacation.

Laci was wearing jeans and a white T-shirt, and she was barefoot, and I couldn't help but notice that she had a perfect, tomato-red pedicure. She was the cutest pregnant woman I had ever seen.

"When I was pregnant, I loved doing my toenails," I told her. "I took great pride in my feet because the rest of me felt so horrible."

Scott was on the far side of the room, sitting in the wheelchair and talking on his cell phone. He was doing little wheelies; I remember wondering whether he'd ever been in a wheelchair himself because he was handling it like an expert.

"Who's he talking to?" I asked Jackie.

"I don't know. A business call. It's always business lately."

This was in November 2002, shortly before Thanksgiving, right around the time he met Amber Frey. I didn't know anything about Amber in those days, of course. This was long before she revealed herself to be the other woman in Scott's life and long before Laci and her unborn son were murdered. And I'm not saying that it was Amber on the phone that afternoon. But I do remember that the following year, I was approached by a pushy reporter, who had some theories of his own: "Scott must have just rolled out of bed with Amber before driving home to Modesto to pick up Laci for that trip to Disneyland," he said.

That horror was still a long way off, and it wasn't something anyone in that room could have imagined. Well, maybe Scott could have; maybe he was imagining it then. The rest of us were busy exchanging gifts, but not Scott. Scott remained on his cell phone, a man apart, in a world of his own.

Jackie had bought me a pair of Burberry gloves, and she had picked up a Burberry scarf for Tim. I had found a Quimper porcelain figure for Jackie: a little angel.

Laci was impressed by my choice. "I can't believe how well you know Jackie already," she said.

"It was easy," I said. "I saw her admiring these at Pierre Deux, in Carmel. I know she collects them."

A moment later, I looked around and couldn't see Ryan, and I began to panic. We were on the fourth floor, and all the windows were open, and I imagined that my little boy had somehow climbed through one of them. For about thirty terrifying seconds, I completely lost it. I ran around the room and in and out of the corridor looking for him and screaming his name. Then Tim called out that he had found him on the balcony—which was certainly frightening enough. He brought him inside and everyone could see that he was fine and we eventually calmed down, but I must say it took my wildly beating heart a while to get back to normal. I looked up and noticed that Scott was still in the wheelchair, still on the cell phone. That struck me as very odd indeed. For thirty seconds everyone in that room had been thrown into a panic by my screams; the entire place was in motion, as Tim, Jackie, Laci, John, Alison—everyone—dashed around looking for Ryan. Only Scott was oblivious.

A short while later we called it a day, said our good-byes, and returned to our rooms to pack. Tim and I and the kids went down to San Diego to spend Thanksgiving with my family, and after a few pleasant days we made the long drive home.

When we arrived in San Francisco, a little note was waiting for us from Jackie. "Thank you for that little angel," she wrote. "May she watch over us all."

She had signed it, "Your fairy godmother."

Laci with Scott at the Latham family reunion

LACI

Laci's baby shower was held on December 10, 2002, in Del Mar, north of San Diego, at a romantic little place called L'Auberge. The hotel, located on a bluff overlooking the Pacific, is one of Jackie's favorite places, as is their French bistro, the Champagne Bakery.

I was in San Diego with my children and my family, and I was so excited for Laci that I overdid it. I bought some colorful baby blocks, several books, a wooden train set, and various baby outfits.

The morning of the party, I was busy wrapping gifts when Ryan came in, looking for trouble. I asked him to help me wrap the gifts, and this seemed to calm him down. "These are for your little cousin, Conner," I said, now that they'd finally decided on a name. "Your Aunt Laci's going to have a baby very soon."

Now that I think back on it, it breaks my heart. My little boy was helping wrap gifts for a cousin he would never meet.

An hour later, my mother and I took Ryan and Tommy and made the short drive north to Del Mar. There were lots of excited hellos and plenty of hugs and kisses, and there was champagne and orange juice in the lobby. Laci's mother and sister had been invited, of course, but they lived many hours to the north, and that side of the family was planning a shower of their own.

When we'd had our fill of the lobby, everyone repaired to a private room, set aside for the occasion, and Laci began opening her gifts. As she did so, I noticed that she was wearing the sapphire cocktail ring I'd asked Jackie to sell for me. I didn't say anything, however. I assumed she had found it in Jackie's house, or at the store, and that she'd borrowed it for the occasion.

Laci was a perfect present-opener. She would look at the card, make eye contact with the person who had brought the gift, read the card aloud, then open the gift and make a few gracious comments about how much she liked it. She was so happy, and so ready to become a mother.

The gifts just never seemed to end. At one point, I remember, Laci opened a box that contained a little blue outfit, and everyone went on and on about how cute it was. Then my mother piped up. "It's so nice when you know the sex of the baby," she said. "I can't stand it when you don't know and have to buy yellow outfits."

The next present was a yellow outfit, and everyone burst out laughing.

• • •

Except for a brief interlude, when my son Ryan decided he would color on the room's pristine walls, the shower went beautifully.

Scott arrived at the very end, but he wasn't his usual gracious self. My mother took a picture of us together, brother and sister, and it was almost as if he was having a hard time holding the smile. Later, when I tried to talk to him, he seemed absent and preoccupied. I thought it might be the shower, that he was overwhelmed in the company of so many women, and I asked him if he was okay.

"Fine," he said, and he turned away. That was so unlike him. This was not the Scott I knew, the one who hung on your every word and made you feel as if you were the center of the universe.

"You must be excited," I suggested.

"Yeah," he said, and he flashed another forced smile, then he went off to see if he could help Laci gather up the gifts and pack them into his truck. He seemed eager to get going.

. . .

Shortly after the shower, I got a card from Laci. "Thank you for the books and toys," she wrote in her impeccable hand. "I can't wait until Conner can play with them and read with Ryan and Tommy." I thought it was a lovely card. I loved the fact that she was already thinking of our boys playing together.

Jackie called that same day to tell me she had received a card as well and to ask if I'd liked mine.

"Yes," I said. "It was lovely. Why?"

"I didn't like the way mine was written," she said.

"What was wrong with it?" I asked.

"It just didn't seem right. It seemed kind of by-the-book."

I never saw the card, and Jackie never volunteered to read it to me, and I couldn't understand why it was so important to her. Maybe Laci had been in a hurry, maybe she was tired, or maybe her back was killing her. But so what? What did that matter?

"I'm going to send her a book on how to write thank you notes," Jackie said.

"Please don't do that," I said. "My card was perfectly lovely. And it'll only upset her. Why upset her when she's so close to having the baby?"

Luckily, Jackie dropped the idea.

. . .

A week later, Jackie called and invited me to Carmel for the night of December 16. She and Lee were going to be there with Laci and Scott, and they had set a room aside for Tim, the kids, and me. Tim was working, and the weather was unpleasant and stormy, and I didn't relish the thought of driving in the rain.

"I just can't do it," I said. "I think I'll pass this time. I'm sorry."

"Don't worry about it," Jackie said, but she sounded disappointed. "I thought it might be fun to spend more time with your brother."

Jackie called almost immediately after the trip to tell me about the bad weather and to complain about her daughter-in-law. "Laci looked so silly," she said. "She was wearing white gloves and a white scarf. She looked like Minnie Mouse."

"You didn't say anything, did you?"

"No, but the next day she wore black gloves and a black scarf, and it wasn't much of an improvement."

I felt awful for Laci. She must have known that Jackie didn't like her outfit—must have seen it in her eyes—and so the next day she went out of her way to please her. I didn't understand why Jackie was having such problems with Laci. I knew that most couples had the usual mother-in-law issues, but hearing this kind of thing from Jackie didn't sit that well with me.

The next time I called Laci, Scott answered the phone and we chatted briefly. I didn't want to say anything about my last conversation with Jackie, but I couldn't help myself, and I told him about this business with the thank you card.

He sighed, exhaling loudly. "Yeah. Those two."

Laci wasn't home, if I remember correctly, so Scott and I chatted for a few more minutes, and I told him that Tim and I and the kids were heading off to Jackson Hole, Wyoming, to spend Christmas with Tim's family. We wished each other a Merry Christmas, and I told him to say hello to Laci.

I had missed my last chance to speak to her.

* * *

We were in Jackson Hole when Laci disappeared.

On Christmas Eve, little Tommy got very sick. He had a chest cold, and he was having a hard time breathing, so we ended up in the emergency room. We were probably overdoing it, but he was only four months old, and I wanted to play it safe.

Then we got back to the family lodge and had dinner and went to bed, and in the morning everyone opened gifts and enjoyed the usual Christmas bedlam.

On December 27, Tim flew home, to Berkeley, and I flew to San Diego for a little post-Christmas celebration with my family. The minute I walked through the door, my mother said that something had happened to Laci, and that Jackie had spoken to Tim and that I should call him right away. I reached him at work, my heart beating like crazy. "What's going on? I asked.

"Laci's been abducted," he said.

"Abducted?" I thought it was a joke. It didn't register. "Abducted by whom? By aliens?"

"Anne," he said firmly. "Laci's missing. Nobody's seen her since Christmas Eve. Everyone is looking for her. You better talk to Jackie. She's in Modesto. Get a pen. I'm going to give you her cell number."

I took the number, feeling numb and lost, and when I got off the phone I felt so nauseated that my mother had to help me to the couch. "What did he say?" she asked.

"He doesn't know anything. He said to call Jackie."

My hands were shaking as I dialed Jackie's number. It still hadn't quite registered—Missing? What did that mean exactly?—but I knew that something was horribly wrong. Laci was family. And she was very pregnant.

"Jackie, it's me."

"Oh, Anne—something awful has happened. No one knows where Laci is. Everyone is trying to find her. The police are all over the place."

I was asking a million questions—What happened? Who saw her last? Where are they looking? What do they think happened?—but they were the same questions that everyone else was asking, and Jackie couldn't tell me much. I could hear people in the background, and I think I recognized Scott's voice, then Jackie said she'd have to call me later and hung up.

I didn't know what to do. My mother showed me a small blurb in the local paper. It said that Laci Denise Peterson, twenty-seven years old and more than eight months pregnant, had been reported missing by her husband, Scott Peterson. It said he came home on Christmas Eve, following a solo fishing trip to the Bay Area, to find the family dog wandering around, a leash still around its neck, but no sign of Laci. Police and volunteers had searched an area called Dry Creek, near Scott and Laci's home, and had combed through East La Loma Park, also near the house, but nothing had turned up.

I felt as if I was slipping into shock. I called Jackie back. "Is there anything I can do to help?" I asked.

"Yes," she said. "Maybe you can stop by the house in Solana Beach. I left without clothes."

I drove north, to the Solana Beach house, and my mother came with me. I found the key in its hiding place, where Jackie had told me it would be, and I unlocked the front door. The place looked as if it had been burglarized. There were clothes all over the floor and the beds were unmade and a half-finished dinner was still on the table, where it had been sitting for three days. Jackie had left in an awful hurry.

I went into her closet and tried to put some outfits together. My mind was sort of half-working. I thought *searching, woods, police,* and it occurred to me that Jackie would need walking shoes and comfortable clothes. I grabbed a few things and asked my mother what she thought. It was crazy: There I was in Jackie's home, with my mother, going through her closets. It felt very strange.

"That's fine," my mother said, and I could see she felt kind of odd about it all, too. "Maybe you can find another sweater. It gets cold at night."

On our way out, I noticed that the answering machine was blinking, and for some crazy reason I thought Jackie should get her messages. I found a pencil and a pad and sat through all eighteen messages, and the experience gave me chills. Many of them were from friends who had heard what had happened and were calling to offer their help and support. "We are so sorry you are going through this. We know things will come out all right. Please call. We are here if you need us." Others were from reporters, who were eager to hear from her and always left three or four contact numbers. And still others were so mundane that they made me feel as if this hadn't really happened. "Hey, Jackie! Just making sure we're still on for breakfast tomorrow at L'Auberge. Call me, honey."

As I was taking messages, my mother began trying to tidy up, somewhat absently, but the moment I was done I told her to leave things as they were, and we locked up and rushed over to the nearest FedEx office. We packed everything into a big box, including the note with the list of phone messages, and shipped it overnight to Scott's house on Covena Avenue, where Jackie was staying.

As we left, I called Jackie to tell her to expect the package, and to see if there was any news. "No," she said, her voice cracking. "They're doing searches and organizing press conferences, and we have a volunteer center, and the police are working nonstop. But no—nothing. So far, nothing."

I asked her how Scott was holding up, and she described his condition in two words: "Not well." I asked if he was there, and if he wanted to talk, and she put him on the phone.

"Anne?" he said, his voice going all croaky.

"I am so sorry this is happening, Scott," I said. "Please let me know what I can do to help. Be strong. I know you can be strong.

They'll find her." I realized that every word out of my mouth was a cliché, but what else could I say?

"Thanks so much," Scott said, his voice still croaky. "This is really hard. You have no idea how hard this is."

By the time I got back to my parents' house, I decided I needed to get home. I felt I needed to be in my own house, in my own neighborhood, where I could regroup and see what I could do to help. I packed up a rented car and put the boys in their car seats and headed north, and of course I couldn't get any of this out of my mind. It was like a home movie playing in my head: *Laci and I meeting for the first time. Laci with her nose buried in pansies. Laci and Scott eating off each other's plates and being wildly in love. Laci at my wedding. Laci in Disneyland. Laci telling me how excited she was about the baby and how ready she was for motherhood.*

Then I remembered how she described floating in the pool to take the pressure off her aching back, and I wondered if the police had looked in the pool. I realized this was an idiotic thought, but I couldn't help myself, and suddenly my mind starting going to some very dark places. I saw Laci tied up in a basement by the people who had abducted her. I saw her, face down in the mud, dead. It played like a horror movie now, and I couldn't seem to stop it.

I put some songs on for the boys, but that didn't do anything to distract me. It just made me think of Conner. Where was little Conner?

• • •

The minute I arrived home, I called Jackie. She still had nothing new to report, and I could hear the pain in her voice. My brother Don had flown out, and he had just arrived at my house with his daughter.

"I feel so useless," I said. "Do you want me to come to Modesto?"

"No," she said. "There're so many people here. It wouldn't help."

"Can we do anything?"

She took a moment and then realized there *was* something we could do. "Yes," she said. "I think so. Could you go down to the Berkeley Marina? The police can't find anyone to verify that Scott was there on the twenty-fourth. Maybe you can find someone who saw him."

We live two miles from the Berkeley Marina; Don and I were there in five minutes. The first person we ran into was a man who lived on his boat. We went up to him and told him that Scott Peterson was our brother. "We're trying to help him," I said. "I wonder if you or anyone you know saw him here on the twenty-fourth." He looked at us, then past us, toward the road, and I noticed a number of people up there.

"There's a lot of reporters around," the man said. "You don't need this." He took a moment and looked off into the distance. "You see that parking lot over there? I'll walk over. You drive. I'll meet you there."

The man was very helpful. In less than an hour he gave us all sorts of information, which I wrote down and took back to the house. We went home and Don sat in front of my computer and typed up the notes, which we then e-mailed to Scott. There were four viable witnesses, and the following is what we took down about each of them:

```
DAVID
David lives on a boat that you pass on your right
when you launch from the marina. He remembers
seeing your truck parked with the trailer and
particularly remembers the toolbox in the truck.
David seems to know everybody at the marina and
is kind of conducting his own mini-investigation.
David has spoken to many of his co-boat owners
about the incident and has much information.
    David has talked to detectives.
```

NICK

We did not speak to Nick directly. Nick apparently lives in the area and frequently visits a boat very close to David's. He also rides his bicycle through the marina area daily. Both Mike [. . .] and David know Nick. Mike believes that Nick did see you launch the boat on the day in question.

Anne was told by Mike or David (not sure which) that Nick had spoken to detectives via telephone.

MIKE

Mike is a groundskeeper who works at the marina. . . . He told us that he specifically remembers you launching the boat in great detail. He stated he remembers you having to back around a white Astro van and hitting the dock and thinking that you probably couldn't see the trailer because the trailer seemed too small for the truck.

Mike has also spoken to detectives.

CLIFF

Cliff is the City of Berkeley supervisor over the groundskeepers and maintenance workers. We did not speak to him directly. Mike [. . .] gave us his name and number.

We obtained a boat launch receipt to check the accuracy of the times. I faxed the receipt to the Red Lion Hotel tonight. I noticed that all the receipts show 11:59 P.M. in large lettering because that is the time all receipts expire on the day they are purchased. The actual purchase

time is shown in smaller letters further up on
the receipt.

Hope this is of some help.

Much later, after the trial, it occurred to me that none of the four
men we e-mailed Scott about that day had been asked to testify. But
when I thought about it, I realized that their testimony wouldn't
have helped Scott. On the contrary, it would have hurt him. The evidence would have placed Scott in the San Francisco Bay—the very
waters in which, months later, passersby would stumble across Laci
and Conner's decomposing bodies.

· · ·

That night, and on every successive night, and often tirelessly
throughout the day, when the kids weren't around, I was glued to the
news. Scott had suddenly become *a person of interest,* in the parlance
of the law and the media, and I was outraged by the suggestion.

So was Jackie. "I can't believe how stupid these reporters are!"
she wailed. "And the police officers! Don't get me started. How can
they let people as unintelligent as that wear a uniform? They don't
know what they're doing! They aren't even looking for Laci. They
should be focusing their efforts on finding her, not pointing fingers
at Scott. How can they even think he had something to do with it?
He was in love. He was in love. You know that. We all know that!
Why aren't they looking for Laci?"

"I guess they're trying," I said, hoping to calm her down. "I saw
on the news that there was a suspicious van in the neighborhood
right around the time she disappeared."

"Yes," Jackie said. "There was also a robbery across the street.

They think it might be connected. And there was a purple car with Confederate flags driving around. People thought it was suspicious."

"So they're doing what they can," I said, trying to bolster her spirits.

"No," she said. "They're not following all the leads. They've been getting dozens of interesting leads at the volunteer center, and the police just aren't following up on any of them."

That night, Jackie and Lee went to Laci's parents' house for dinner. I'm sure nobody ate. I can't even imagine what they talked about.

The next morning, my brother Don said something that really bothered me: "How well do you know Scott?" he asked.

"What do you mean?"

"Nothing. It's just a question. You live here. You vacation with them. You know Scott a lot better than I do. Jackie says you and he are very close."

"We are close," I said. But I didn't say anything else. I didn't even want to entertain the notion that Scott might have had something to do with Laci's disappearance. I wasn't going to go there. Everyone else was, but not me. Plus I didn't want to think that anything bad had happened to Laci. I loved Laci. There were so many things we were going to do together. We had our whole lives ahead of us.

Still, it was clear that more and more people were beginning to wonder about Scott. On December 30, police arrived at Scott's place with a search warrant and spent several hours going through the house. They took two computers, along with Laci's SUV and Scott's pickup truck.

The next night, December 31, about a thousand people attended a candlelight vigil for Laci in East La Loma Park. I didn't go. I stayed home with Tim and the kids and watched it on TV. Ryan asked me what we were watching, and I turned off the TV and told him, "Nothing."

"I saw Aunt Laci," he said.

"What do you mean?" I asked, chilled to the bone.

"I saw her picture."

Of course. He had seen one of the posters.

. . .

On January 2, the police asked for the public's help in verifying Scott's alibi. He had receipts related to his fishing trip, and the police were looking for anyone who had actually seen him, either at the Berkeley Marina or out on the water.

I didn't understand this. I wondered if Scott had shared the information I had e-mailed him, and I was doubly confused because several of the men I spoke to told me they had already been questioned by detectives. I called Jackie to ask her about it.

"Of course we gave them the e-mail," she said. "I told you. They're idiots."

She was beginning to panic, to lash out at anyone who didn't seem to be on her side, and I honestly can't say I blamed her. This was her son they were talking about, her little boy. This was one of the children she had kept.

I continued to watch the news and read the papers, hoping I'd stumble across the one clue that would break the case wide open. At one point, I decided to investigate on my own. I got on the computer and Googled the words "missing," "pregnant," and "women." The first batch of stories was all about Laci, of course, but as I scrolled down I discovered stories about five missing pregnant women in Northern California alone. One of the missing was Evelyn Hernandez, a pregnant twenty-four-year-old who had disappeared with her five-year-old son, Alex. A month later someone found her wallet, with the money still inside, and in July her remains were discovered in the San Francisco Bay. According to the account I read, the case remained under investigation.

On January 11, police divers searched the San Francisco Bay.

One of the local channels said they had made a discovery related to Laci's disappearance, and I was a nervous wreck for several hours. Later the reporter changed his story, saying the police had been mistaken. I was furious—not at the police, but at the fact that the station had aired the story with no regard for Laci's friends and family. To them, that's all Laci was: a story. To us, she was a person we loved, and every moment without her was torture.

• • •

The next day was Tommy's christening. It had been planned well in advance, and I didn't think it made much sense to cancel it. In fact, I thought I should invite Jackie, Lee, and Scott, and I reached Jackie on her cell and suggested they drive up. "We're only an hour and a half from Modesto," I said. "It might be good to get away for a little while. And I don't know how you feel about such things, but you might even want to talk to the priest."

They agreed to come. I went on ahead of them, to St. Clement's Episcopal Church on Claremont Boulevard in Berkeley, and explained our situation to the rector. He was very understanding. He said he would be glad to talk to the family after the service, if they were inclined to talk to him, but he wanted to leave it up to them. He didn't want to put them on the spot by suggesting it.

A short time later, Scott, Jackie, and Lee arrived in a rented car. I went out to greet them. I hadn't seen Scott since before Laci's disappearance, and I was nervous. The first words out of my mouth were about the car. "Is it new?"

"No," Scott said. "They took my truck."

I knew this, of course, but I was flustered. I gave Scott a little kiss and said hello to Jackie and Lee, and we walked toward the church.

"How're you holding up?" I asked Scott.

"I'm not," he said. "This is a nightmare."

He was wearing a nice suit, and he had even taken the time to put a little gel in his hair, which was not something I'd ever seen him do. I thought that was a little odd, but I didn't say anything. Scott followed me into church and said hello to Tim and the rest of the family; he was low-key and cordial, like the old Scott. I asked him to hold Tommy during the christening, and Scott thanked me for the honor and took my baby from my arms. Afterward, he sat next to me during the short service. He kept turning in his seat, looking toward one of the pews near the back, and when I turned to look I saw a man sitting there alone. He had dark hair and a mustache, and he was looking straight ahead, not at Scott and not at me. There was no expression on his face. I assumed he was a detective.

As soon as the service was over, I told Scott and Jackie that the rector was very nice and that maybe we should talk to him for a few minutes. I believe in God, and I thought it might be helpful. The rector took us back to his private quarters, and Lee was the first to speak. "What is someone to do in a situation like this?" he asked, his voice cracking. I looked and saw tears in his eyes and suddenly felt tears spilling down my cheeks. Lee remained on his feet. "How does one get through it?"

"There's really nothing you can do," the rector said gently. "Laci is in God's hands."

Then Jackie spoke up. She was in pain, but she was also angry and frustrated, and she started listing all the things she and the family were doing to help. Searching. Putting up posters. Holding vigils. Going door-to-door to question people. She preferred talking about all this to talking about her feelings. Clearly, this was one way of dealing with the pain, by not dealing with it, not facing it.

I looked over at Scott. He was holding Tommy again, and when our eyes met he began to cry. He just kept staring at me, with those big tears in his eyes, and it made me very uncomfortable. I got the feeling that he was trying to tell me something, and it frightened me. I looked away, at the rector. I know he had seen the tears in

Scott's eyes, too, but he was not looking at him now. In fact, he had turned away from him, as if he didn't want to acknowledge Scott, as if he saw something there he didn't like.

This bothered me immensely. This was a man of God; I thought that he, of all people, should be reaching out to Scott, and he wasn't. Instead he just bowed his head and said a little prayer for Laci, and then he looked up to see if he could do anything else for us. Once again, it seemed to me that he was making a concerted effort to *not* look at Scott.

Jackie stood up and thanked the rector for his time and the rest of us followed her out. We reconvened a few minutes later for brunch at the Claremont Hotel. It was an odd group: Scott, Jackie, Lee, Susan and her boyfriend, and Tim and I and the two boys. I missed my parents, who were away in Europe, and I really missed Laci, whose absence was so palpable. It was actually very strange to be there without her, and even stranger that no one spoke about her or about the case.

After brunch, Susan and Jim took off and I walked Scott and his parents back to their car and wished them well. When I rejoined Tim and the boys, he looked at me and said, "That was really freaky."

"What?" I asked.

"The service. Brunch. Having him around. Didn't that freak you out?"

"No," I said. "Why would it freak me out? He's my brother. I know he didn't have anything to do with this."

Many months later, I discovered two things about that day that *did* freak me out. One of them concerned Scott's cable service. According to evidence presented at the trial, Scott called his cable provider that very afternoon and had two hard-core porn channels added to his account.

Also that afternoon, Scott called Amber Frey, who was taping their conversations for the police, and spoke to her about his faith in God. "I've got my Bible in front of me," he told her, and he quoted from Luke 8:4–8: And when much people were gathered together, and were come to him out of every city, he spake by a parable: A sower went out to sow his seed: and as he sowed, some fell by the way side; and it was trodden down, and the fowls of the air devoured it. And some fell upon a rock; and as soon as it was sprung up, it withered away, because it lacked moisture. And some fell among thorns; and the thorns sprang up with it, and choked it. And other fell on good ground, and sprang up, and bare fruit an hundredfold."

"I need to get some good soil for us," he told Amber, sounding like a man who was planning his future. "I need to get some good soil for us."

• • •

A week later, long before I knew any of this, long before I had any doubts at all about my little brother, he called from Modesto.

"Hey Sis," he said.

"Hey," I said. "How you doing?"

"Mom asked me to call you," he said.

"Yeah?"

"She wants to know if maybe I could stay with you guys."

"Oh?"

"I'm being hounded out of Modesto. The police, the press, people on the street. I've got to get out of here."

Jackie took the phone from him. "Can you help us, Anne? He needs to get out of here. He needs to be with family in a place where nobody can find him. He's just so sad and broken. He'll never want to come back to this house now. Laci will never want to come back. This place is finished for them."

Scott took the phone back. "Mom's right, Anne. Would you mind if I crashed there for a while? I promise I won't be in the way. Would you mind very much if I stayed with you guys?"

No, I didn't mind. I didn't mind at all. He was my brother. I believed in him. The family would get through this together.

An open window in the room in our home that Scott stayed in

SAFE HAVEN

Scott had been at our place in Berkeley two or three times, mostly passing through on business. On his last visit, however, he had been there to do a favor for Jackie and Lee. They had bought a small cabin in the Sierras—the doctors felt the mountain air might be good for Jackie's lungs—and they needed to furnish it. Tim and I were replacing some of our old furniture, and they sent Scott to pick it up. The two men loaded it into the truck and Scott drove off into the foothills the following morning, eager to deliver it.

Now he was back, under very different circumstances, and he was a changed man—changed mostly by the horror of the preceding weeks. When he walked in I gave him a big hug and kiss, and Ryan hurried over to say hello to his Uncle Scott.

He looked exhausted, understandably, and he began by thanking me for putting him up. "You can't believe what it's like down there," he said. "I'm basically a prisoner of my own face. Everywhere I go, people stare at me." He shook his head. "I can't go anywhere, I can't do anything, and I've got nothing left. The police took everything. Even my computers."

I took him upstairs and showed him the room where he'd be staying. It's a loft, and it overlooks the San Francisco Bay, with the Bay Bridge visible in the distance. The loft is quite cozy. It has parchment-painted, angled ceilings, and there were floral Ralph

Lauren sheets on the bed. A rolltop desk stood against one wall. Everything looked right. I found myself thinking that Laci would probably like the room. She would have found some way to improve it, no doubt, but she would have liked it.

I turned to look at Scott and noticed that he had the beginnings of a goatee. "So what's this?" I asked.

"Nothing," he said, rubbing his chin. "Just seeing how it looks."

When we went back downstairs, I noticed his truck outside. I was confused because I'd heard that the police had taken his truck, so either they'd returned it, or he'd borrowed one from a friend. And I was doubly confused by what he said next: "The cops put a tracking device on that thing."

"They did?"

"Yeah."

"How do you know?"

"Because I saw it under the seat but couldn't get it out. And those guys can find me anywhere. Every time I look in my rearview mirror, there they are."

Scott fooled around with Ryan a bit, roughhousing on the couch, and then Tim came home and they greeted each other and I went into the kitchen to make dinner. Tim wasn't being particularly friendly, but he wasn't being hostile, either. I'd asked him if it was okay for Scott to stay with us, and he wasn't exactly thrilled, but he wanted to do the right thing. After all, Scott was family.

After I got the boys to bed, we sat down and I broke out a couple of nice zinfandels. I wanted Scott to feel relaxed, to know that he was safe here, and we didn't get into anything about Laci or the continuing investigation. We talked about wines, and the relative merits of one zinfandel over another, and we polished off two bottles among the three of us.

Scott didn't look particularly tortured; in fact, as the evening went on he seemed to get a second wind. Suddenly he was chatting and smiling like a guy who didn't have a care in the world. I thought it might be the wine, and I also thought he deserved a break, so I accepted it. Still, it had been several weeks now since Laci had disappeared, and I couldn't even begin to imagine what he must be going through. And even now, as I'm putting these words to paper, I realize just how right I was: I could not even begin to imagine the horrible images that would remain forever in his head.

That night, I got Scott situated in the loft and went off to prepare for bed. Tim was already under the covers, but he was wide awake. He looked at me.

"What?"

"Are you at all bothered by this?"

"By what?"

"By him. By having him here."

"No," I said. "I'm not going to be like everyone else. The whole world assumes he's guilty."

"That should tell you something."

"It doesn't tell me anything," I said. "The whole world doesn't know him like I know him."

"What was it your brother Don said? 'How well do you know Scott?' Isn't that what he said?"

"You know something, Tim? I'm not going to argue with you. In this country, people are innocent until proven guilty. I know Scott pretty well. I know that he is not capable of doing something so horrible, and I'm not even going to go there."

I remembered some of those nightmarish images I'd struggled with that day after the news broke, and I did my best to put them out of my mind.

"I don't know," Tim said. "I sort of expected him to be more screwed up over this. He seemed fine at dinner. He seemed like a guy who didn't have a care in the world."

"He was making an effort to be sociable," I said.

"It didn't look like it took much effort."

"It was the wine, then," I snapped, unable to keep the anger from my voice. "Is that what you want to hear? It was the wine."

And so it began: the big sister, making excuses for her little brother.

. . .

The next day, Scott went into town and picked up some new clothes at REI and The North Face. He told me the police had taken most of his clothes, and that he'd left in a hurry, so he didn't even have time to pack the few things that they'd left. He sat on the couch with his purchases, removing the tags and watching himself on TV. There was a recent shot of him making his way down a Modesto street. I could tell it was recent because he had the new goatee.

"So what do you think, Sis?" he asked, rubbing his chin. "You think I should get rid of this thing?"

"I don't know," I said. "It looks okay to me."

I wasn't really thinking about the goatee, but I was wondering why *he* was thinking about it. Scott sat there watching himself on TV, listening to reporters talking about his missing wife, dissecting the case, scrambling for new developments . . . and he seemed more interested in his new facial hair than in the search for his wife. Then he turned his attention back to the TV and began to shake his head.

"They're looking in the wrong places," he said.

"Who?"

"The police. Everyone."

A normal response would have been to ask him where they should be looking, but I didn't ask him. I didn't want to know why he knew that they were looking in the wrong places or where he might suggest they should be looking. But it gnawed at me. And it kept gnawing at me.

*   *   *

The next day our babysitter, whom I'll call Lorraine, came to help me with the kids. She is very attractive, and when Scott saw her he did a double take. Suddenly he was smiling and flirting. He was now a *very* long way from the bereaved husband. He looked like a charming young man without a care in the world—a man on the make.

Our babysitter was a little uncomfortable, but I found myself wondering whether part of her liked the attention.

After she left, Scott couldn't help himself. "That is one very pretty babysitter," he declared.

"Yes," I replied. "And she lives with her handsome young boyfriend."

We went into town and picked up some groceries and a few bottles of wine. Jackie had called to ask me how Scott was doing and to tell me that he was broke and whether I would mind helping out a bit. I told her that he seemed to be happy at our place and that I'd make sure he got plenty to eat.

That night, we had dinner again—Tim, Scott, and I—and we washed it down with two bottles of wine. When we turned on the TV, the news was on, and, as always, it was about Laci. Reporters were going on about the various searches, and it was mostly stuff we'd already heard, but I was riveted. This wasn't simply a news story. This was a news story that involved people I loved, and one of the principal players was sitting right here, in my living room. Scott wasn't even looking at the TV, which I found a little irksome. If anything, he should be hungry for details. If it was me, I would be doing everything in my power to find my missing wife. I'd be obsessed to the point of madness.

I went and found an area map and spread it out on the table.

"What are you doing?" Scott asked.

"I'm just trying to get some ideas about where she might be," I said.

Scott got a bored look on his face. I saw it, and Tim saw it, and Tim got up and found another bottle of wine and went to look for the opener. I ignored him and turned my attention back to the map. "Did they ever find out about that car with the Confederate flags?" I asked Scott. "Or the van?"

"I don't know," Scott said, and it seemed as if talking to me took incredible effort. "I think the van belonged to some landscape guy. The car I don't know about."

I heard the pop of the cork, followed by the gurgling of wine being poured. Tim was behind me, and I couldn't see him, but from the sounds of it he was pouring himself a very generous glass. This was unusual for us. We like a little wine now and again, but we had been overdoing it since Laci's disappearance, and Tim always seemed to be way ahead of me.

"Let me have a little of that," Scott said.

Tim set the bottle on the table, where Scott could reach it, and Scott refilled his glass.

"Just look at the map, Scott," I said. "Just take a guess. You knew Laci. Is there someplace here she liked? Someplace that jumps out at you? Someplace the police might have missed?"

Scott looked at me like he was on the verge of getting angry, and I got the feeling he was doing his best to contain himself. He raised his finger and very theatrically brought it down in an area near Modesto, right around Interstate 5. "Here," he said. "Yes. Maybe here. I think that's a place they haven't looked."

The way he said it was patronizing, bordering on nasty. It seemed as if he had picked the spot at random just to shut me up. I looked closer, where his finger had been. "Mape's Ranch?" I asked. "What is that? Does that place mean anything to you and Laci?"

"We've been past it," Scott said dismissively. He got up and moved to a more comfortable chair and stretched out his legs. I saw Tim looking at me. He was pissed. He brought his wine to his lips and drained the glass and went off to the bedroom. I looked over at Scott. He was studying the color of his wine, holding it up to the light. He seemed like a man without a care in the world.

But I was wrong. He had his cares. According to evidence introduced in court at his trial, on January 14 he was talking to his girlfriend, Amber Frey, about the things that really mattered to a man like him—the things he cared about. "I really care about you," he had told her, "so communication is precious to me."

The following day, January 15, the police went to see Laci's parents. They told Sharon Rocha and Ron Grantski that Scott had been having an affair with a woman from Fresno, but they stopped short of identifying Amber Frey by name. They also told them that Scott had recently taken out a $250,000 life insurance policy on Laci.

Laci's parents didn't share this information with Jackie—maybe they had been asked to keep it to themselves—so the Peterson side of the family was left in the dark.

• • •

Scott came and went as he pleased, and I gave him a key to the house. This really upset Tim. "What do you want me to do?" I asked. "He's my brother."

"I know he's your brother," he snapped. "You keep saying that."

"I'm sorry. I don't know what else to say."

He was getting ready to go out—I think it was a Saturday—and I grabbed the kids and we all went out together. We ended up at an auction house in Oakland, a place Tim likes to go to. He collects clocks, and he's always looking for new ones. We didn't see any clocks that day, but I saw something that gave me a bit of a jolt. It was a pair of platinum earrings with screw-backs. They looked exactly like a pair I'd seen on Laci some months back. I was so shaken that I asked to talk to the person in charge of jewelry, and when she came out I identified myself as Laci's sister-in-law. She was both taken aback and sympathetic, and when I explained about the earrings she rushed to her office to look at her records. A few minutes later, still looking flustered, she was back. "The people we got those earrings from are very reliable people," she said. "We've been doing business with them for many years. Also, I should point out that those aren't one-of-a-kind earrings. It's possible that they just look like the ones your sister-in-law was wearing. If you could come back with a more exact description, however, I will do everything I can to help. And if anything matches up, we'll involve the police."

When we got home, I called Jackie and told her about the earrings. She asked me to call Sharon Rocha and tell her the story. I had never met Sharon Rocha, and I felt a little awkward about calling, but I took the number and called anyway. I left a message. I told her I was Scott's sister, and I apologized for bothering her, but I thought this might be important. I described the earrings and told her what I'd discussed with the woman at the auction house, and I gave her my phone number.

I didn't hear back from her, and I was disappointed. Laci had wanted me to meet her mother, and we had talked about it several times, but it never happened. That was probably my fault. I had never gone to Modesto to visit Laci.

When I called Jackie back to tell her I'd left a message, I ended up talking to Lee. He sounded very upset. "It sickens me," he said. "It seems that every day Scott is becoming more and more of a suspect in people's minds. I don't know how they can suspect him. What has he done that makes them so suspicious?" Lee was a man of few words, but he was talking now. "What is he supposed to do?

Me as a playful two-year-old, with my adopted parents, Jerri and Tom Grady

With my fiancé, Tim Bird, in 1998

At Laci's baby shower. *Clockwise from top left:* Alison, Jennifer, and Janey Peterson, me, Laci, and Susan (Lee's daughter).

The San Francisco Bay—where Laci and Conner were eventually found—as seen from the loft bedroom in our house where Scott stayed during the search (inset).

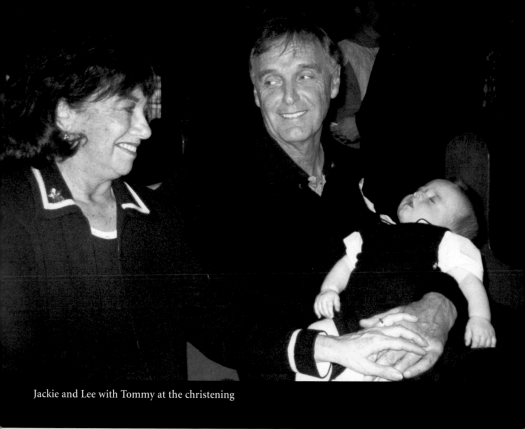
Jackie and Lee with Tommy at the christening

MISSING
$500,000 REWARD
(For information leading to a safe return)
Laci Peterson
Age: 27, Ht. 5'1"
Brown Hair & Brown Eyes
Any information, Please Call
342-6166

The change in location forces the move to letters to communicate. Access to a common-room, between cells here is twice a day,

1/26/04

Dear Anne,

I yearn to communicate with my missed sister, but hesitate to write. I feel puerile in the appearance of this correspond-ence; caused by the "elegant" stubby number two pencil I am forced to use (it is lengthened by a rolled piece of aces taped to it's end) and the juvenile formation of my handwriting. The first letter scrawled, the "d" in dear, is an inauspicious start. I have decided

9470&+2012

in the morning in the evening. I am curious to see what happens this evening as my "rec" time this morning somehow extended to over an hour. Was that my time for the entire day? I assume it was a mistake and choose not to question

2.

sealed desk.
Remember, this letter asks in its statements for reciprocity.

With Love,
Scott

They hate him because he isn't showing emotion. But if he was showing emotion, maybe they'd say he was overdoing it."

"You're right," I said. "There's just no rule book for this. Nobody knows how you're supposed to behave in these types of situations."

"How *is* he supposed to behave?" he replied. "Can anyone tell me that? How in God's name is he supposed to behave?"

He sounded traumatized, and I was doing my best to help, but it didn't seem as if I was getting through to him.

Jackie, meanwhile, was also struggling. But unlike Lee, who tended to internalize his feelings, she began lashing out at everyone in sight, especially the police. They were incompetent. They weren't making an effort to find Laci. They were treating her son as if he was somehow involved in Laci's disappearance.

I didn't know how to help them, and it saddened me. I had only recently rediscovered my family, and they had become an integral part of my life, and suddenly we had been visited by horror and tragedy.

· · ·

In late January, Tim and I took the kids to Mexico for a few days. We thought it would be good for them and good for us. The tragedy was beginning to drive a wedge between us, and it was compounded by Scott's presence, by the way he was using our home as a hotel. I wanted to handle the problem before it was too late. I was also worried about Tim. It was impossible to miss his frustration and unhappiness, and I worried, with all of our sitting around drinking wine at night, that neither one of us was dealing with it at all.

On January 21, while we were in Mexico, a Modesto newspaper claimed that Scott had been having an affair. It also mentioned the $250,000 life insurance policy on Laci's life. When Scott was questioned by a passing TV reporter about the report, he called the allegations "a bunch of lies."

When I reached Jackie on the phone, she was livid. She hated that cow town, hated the reporters, and hated the police. "But I spoke to Diane Sawyer," she added, as if that were a good thing. I didn't think it was a good thing. I thought she and the family should keep as low a profile as possible. By this time, Laci's disappearance had become a national story. The press saw that it had all the right elements: a handsome young businessman on the rise, his beautiful, smiling wife, and the baby they were expecting. This was a far cry from the usual sordid murder stories. The press seemed to be saying, *These are nice people. These are people like us. Our kind of people.* And audiences ate it up. As a result, there didn't seem to be anyone who wasn't aware of Laci. The story didn't need any more publicity. I didn't think a call from Diane Sawyer was anything to celebrate.

"She wants to talk to us and Scott," Jackie said.

"I don't know," I said. "Is that such a good idea?"

• • •

On Janaury 23, the Rochas gave a news conference at the Modesto Police Department. Amy Rocha, Laci's younger half sister, was the first to speak. "The past few weeks have been the most painful I've ever experienced," she said, but she couldn't go on. Then Laci's older brother, Brent, took the microphone. When he announced that the family had lost faith in Scott, I was completely floored. "I trusted him and stood by him in the initial phases of my sister's disappearance," he said. "However, Scott has not been forthcoming with information regarding my sister's disappearance, and I'm only left to question what else he may be hiding."

Finally, it was Sharon Rocha's turn. It was odd seeing the family there in the Modesto police station: Sharon, Amy, Brent, and, in the background, Ron Grantski. These were people I'd often heard about from Laci, and in a strange way I almost felt as if they were my in-laws. "Since Christmas Eve, our one and only focus has been to find Laci and bring her home to us," Sharon said. "I love my daughter so much. I miss her every minute of every day. I miss seeing her. I miss our talking together. I miss listening to the excitement in her voice when she talks to me about her baby. I miss not being able to share with her the anticipation of her approaching delivery date. I miss listening to her talk about her future with her husband and her baby. I miss sharing our thoughts and our lives together. I miss her smile and her laughter and her sense of humor. And I miss everything about her.

"Someone has taken all of this away from me and everyone else who loves her. There are no words that can possibly describe the ache in my heart or the emptiness in my life."

I was crying long before she finished, and I was still crying long after she was done.

• • •

The next day, January 24, it was Amber Frey's turn. I sat glued to the television, my mouth open.

"Okay, first of all, I met Scott Peterson on November 20 of 2002," she said. "I was introduced to him. I was told he was unmarried. Scott told me he was not married. We did have a romantic relationship."

The hits just kept on coming.

"When I discovered he was involved in the Laci Peterson disappearance case, I immediately contacted the Modesto Police Department," she continued.

"Although I could have sold the photos of Scott and I to the tabloids, I knew this was not the right thing to do. For fear of jeopardizing the case or the investigation, I will not comment further."

She seemed very shaken, and for a moment she looked completely lost. But then she pulled herself together and finished what she had to say: "I am very sorry for Laci's family and the pain that this has caused them. And I pray for her safe return, as well.

"I would appreciate (if) my friends and acquaintances (would) refrain from talking about me to the media for profit or recognition. I am a single mother with a twenty-three-month-old child, and I ask [you] to respect my privacy. Thank you."

Tim was watching this with me, and when Amber had finished I could feel his eyes on me. I was almost afraid to look at him.

"What do you think now?" he asked.

"I don't know. He was having an affair. It doesn't mean he hurt Laci."

"Are you kidding me?!" He was furious. "Are you honestly going to tell me you believe he's innocent?"

"Tim, I don't know what I believe anymore."

"Well that Amber girl isn't lying!" he shot back. "Why would she lie? You don't go to the police and make up a story about having an affair with some guy who forgot to tell you he was married, and you especially don't go to them if the guy's wife is missing."

"What are you saying?"

"I'm saying you better start doing some serious thinking about your little brother."

"What do you want me to do, Tim?"

"I don't want him in our house."

"That's not fair. He has nowhere else to go."

"You're not his only family, okay? He's got other family. You wouldn't even know about him if that Don guy hadn't shown up with this 'great news' about your birth mother."

That was low. He had me in tears now. Instead of apologizing, he went off to get a drink. When he came back, I told him I wasn't going to abandon Scott. "After this, everyone's going to turn on him. He needs us."

"I don't want him in my house. I don't want him around my kids."

"Why don't we give him a chance to explain?"

"He's a pathological liar. Maybe worse. What's he going to tell you? 'Hey Sis, I didn't do it?'"

"So you're just going to assume he's guilty?"

"I don't think it was the guy with the Confederate flags, okay? Or the burglars across the street."

"Do you think Laci's dead?"

"Of course I think Laci's dead. Everyone thinks Laci's dead. Everyone but you."

He was right. I didn't know what to do anymore. Even Laci's family had turned on Scott. What had they seen that I wasn't seeing? Or, more accurately, what was I refusing to see?

"Don't you want to hear it from him?"

"No! I told you. I don't want him in our house."

"I'm not putting him out in the street, Tim. I can't do that."

My cell phone rang. We both looked at it. I went over and picked it up. It was Jackie. I hadn't spoken to her in two days, since the day before Laci's family held their news conference.

"Have you been watching the news?" she asked, beside herself.

"Yes."

"That Sharon Rocha, there's a word to describe that woman. She is evil. That's what she is, *evil*. She and her friends and family are destroying my son. How dare they stand there and point the finger at Scott?! Who do they think they are? As for that Amber Frey, what's the big deal? So Scott slept with a bimbo? So what?"

She was pretty worked up, and Lee took the phone from her. "Anne, don't worry. Jackie's very upset. But she's right. Men stray sometimes. It doesn't mean Scott hurt Laci. He wouldn't have hurt Laci."

When I got off the phone, Tim was staring at me.

"What?"

"What did she say?"

"She's mad at Laci's family. And Lee said not to jump to conclusions. Sometimes men just stray."

"You know what? They *do* stray. But I don't think very much of a man like that."

I knew this was hard for Tim. Tim had liked Scott from the start, and Tim prides himself on being a good friend. He has solid values. He was also brought up to believe that a man doesn't cheat on his wife. If a man has a problem, and the marriage isn't working, and he doesn't think it will ever work, he should get out. But to start up with another woman while you're still married was plain wrong.

"Okay," I said. "He cheated on her, and it's wrong. But like Lee said, it doesn't mean he hurt Laci."

"He's a coward. He's a coward, and he's a cheat. And brother or no brother, I think he's much worse."

"I just can't believe that about Scott," I said.

"Why?"

"Because I can't."

"He cheated on Laci. He lied to all of us. Then he comes to our house and whines about the way he's being treated by the press and by the police and by people on the streets, but when do you ever hear him talking about Laci? When has he said he misses Laci? When have you seen him break down?"

How could I argue with that? I couldn't. And yet I tried.

I didn't want to believe that Scott was capable of hurting Laci. He was my flesh and blood. It wasn't in him. Was it?

94

*   *   *

The next time I saw Scott, I came right out and asked him. "I want to know about Amber," I said.

"She's nothing," he said. "It was just a fling. Down and dirty. It meant nothing."

"I don't understand. . . ."

"It happens, okay?" he said, cutting me off. "People cheat. Don't act like people never cheat. I mean, I remember one time on this long flight—I took turns with two women in two separate bathrooms. And another time—there was this girl in San Luis Obispo. It was just sex. Nothing else."

I didn't know why he was telling me this. All I could think was that he was trying to trivialize that sordid business with Amber.

"Did Laci know?" I ventured to ask.

"Yes!" he said dismissively, turning away to avoid my eyes. "And she was extremely pissed off, okay?" He looked back at me now, as if he were trying to gauge my response—as if he wanted to see whether I believed him. "She'll get through it," he added. "She's been through it before. It was no big deal."

At this point I knew he was lying, so I didn't pursue it.

"What are you going to do?" I asked him.

"Nothing," he said, disappearing in the direction of the loft. "It's just as well people know. Now we can concentrate on what really matters."

I went out to buy groceries, and when I came back he was gone. I remember that Scott had used our computer, and I wondered if there was anything on it. He had a Hotmail account and his password was "biscuit," or "biscuitluv," his nicknames for Laci, but I didn't know how to access his account.

When I looked at the recent history on our computer, I saw that someone had been looking at porn. It upset me. I decided to stop digging.

. . .

Jackie was calling again, and soon her calls were coming nonstop. I was hearing from her two or three times a day, and it was always the same litany of complaints, only harsher and angrier.

"Those Rochas—what awful people!"

"No one is standing up for Scott. I thought this was America. Where's the justice?"

"Why are they looking in the bay? Just because Scott went fishing there? What do they think they're going to find in the bay?"

"My son has done nothing wrong!"

Sometimes, after I got off the phone with her, I would call my parents in San Diego. Just as Jackie turned to me for support, I would turn to them. My father was noncommittal. He would listen politely, saying little, but I could tell he was worried about me and about my involvement in the case. He never breathed a word about Scott's guilt or innocence, however.

My mother was equally supportive and a very patient listener. I would find myself telling her stories about Laci, suddenly remembering little things I myself had forgotten. Most of them were inconsequential. I told her how Laci had wanted a new car, not for herself, but for the baby, and how she was on this mission to find the safest car in the world. I told her about that time in Disneyland when we'd laughed about my thirty-dollar plumping lipstick. And I remembered the way she'd rolled her eyes when we walked into Pierre Deux.

"Are you okay, honey?" my mother asked

"Yes," I said.

"Are you sure?"

"I miss Laci."

"I know, honey."

"I miss her a lot."

"You're sure you're okay?"

"Yes," I said. But I wasn't okay. Laci was gone, Scott's behavior was becoming increasingly bizarre, Jackie was falling apart, and my marriage to Tim was showing the strain. "I'm fine."

• • •

It was right around then that Jackie and Lee approached Kirk McAllister about representing Scott. The next time Scott came by the house—unannounced, as always—I asked him about McAllister. "Do you like him?" I asked.

"Yeah," he said. "He seems like a nice guy."

I didn't think "nice" was the issue. I told Scott I had a friend who was married to a criminal lawyer and that I could probably arrange for them to meet. "It would be informal," I said. "If you have some questions, he might be able to answer them. You never know. It could help."

Scott wasn't exactly enthusiastic about the idea, but he didn't seem to object to it, so I invited the lawyer over and left him alone with Scott and a couple of beers. They talked for about an hour, and when they were done I walked the lawyer out. I wanted to ask him what he thought of Scott, and he could see what was coming, and he was very professional about it. "It's better if you don't ask," he said. "It wouldn't be right."

I went back into the house, and Scott didn't volunteer anything either. He was sitting there with a fresh beer, acting as if the last hour had never happened.

"How'd you like him?" I asked.

"Good guy," he said. "Thanks for setting that up."

That was all I got from him, so the next day I went to see my friend, the attorney's wife, and I cornered her in her kitchen. "I'm dying to know what he told you," I said.

She said she didn't know anything and that she couldn't tell me even if she did. It would have been a violation of Scott's rights. But in my heart I knew; the look on the lawyer's face was enough. He must have thought Scott had had something to do with it. If he thought otherwise, he wouldn't have been so quick to run off; he would have stuck around for a second beer.

I know I looked tortured because my friend seemed very concerned and asked me if I was okay.

"I don't know," I said.

"Well, what do you think, Anne? Do you think Scott had something to do with this?"

"I don't know," I repeated. But I realized I'd begun to waver. "I don't even want to think about it. If I really believed he was capable of hurting Laci . . ." I trailed off then tried again. "If I really believed he was capable of hurting Laci, the world would seem like a much, much darker place."

When I got home, Scott and Tim were sitting in front of the television, watching an old movie. They both looked up as I came through the door, their heads moving in slow motion. Scott half-waved. Tim didn't even do that much.

I heard Scott climbing toward the loft later that evening. Tim never made it to the bedroom.

In the morning, surprisingly, Scott was gone. I had expected him to spend the day in bed, nursing a hangover. I saw him again that night, on television. He was talking about the case with Gloria Gomez, a local reporter. I had no idea when he had done the interview, nor whether what I was watching was a new piece or a repeat. But I do know it was very disturbing.

Scott began by talking about how he went through "a range of emotions, from anger to frustration to grief," and how they came and went at different times of the day. I'd seen a little frustration, and I'd seen a little anger, but I hadn't really seen much grief. The only time I had seen Scott cry was at Tommy's christening, and there had been something off-putting about those tears.

Under continued questioning, he went on to explain why he went fishing on his own on the day that Laci disappeared, despite the fact that it was Christmas Eve and that there was so much to do. Everything was already taken care of, he said, and Laci was fine with his going. The two of them had "separate pursuits. . . . It's the way our relationship works."

Ms. Gomez then asked him about Amber—thinking, perhaps, that she was one of Scott's "pursuits"—and he told her he was relieved when Amber came forward. "I'm glad she did the press conference. I'm glad that's out there. It had nothing to do with Laci's disappearance."

When I heard Scott tell Gomez that Laci had known about the affair, I practically fell out of my seat. He said Laci knew not because she found out, but because he, Scott, had volunteered the information. Asked why he had done so, Scott said, "Just because it was the right thing to do. As you know, when you're not doing the right thing, it just, you know, eats you up. . . . You feel . . . sick to your stomach, and you can't function, and . . . you have a hard time, you know, looking at someone."

That was a blatant lie. Laci couldn't have known that Scott was having an affair. If she had, she wouldn't have kept it to herself. She may have been concerned about image and about appearances but not to the point of madness. Laci would have shared her heartbreak with someone—if not me, then with the mother she loved, or with any number of the close friends she often talked about.

The next thing I knew, Scott was showing the reporter his

hands. "You can see cuts here on my knuckles, numerous scars," he said. "I work on farms. I work with machinery. I know I cut my knuckle on that day . . . on Christmas Eve . . . reaching in the tool-box in my truck and then into the pocket on the door. I cut open my knuckle and there was a bloodstain on the door."

This was getting altogether too bizarre; now we were in O. J. Simpson territory. The reporter was asking the same questions that were on everyone's mind: Why had he gone fishing on his own? What about that life insurance policy? Was there anything to the rumors about blood evidence? She also wanted him to explain something I was hearing about for the first time: What had happened to the fifty pounds of cement mix that Scott had purchased at Home Depot around the time of Laci's disappearance? Scott almost lost his temper: "I'm not going to waste what little time we have . . . by defending myself against irrelevant things."

But I didn't think they were irrelevant. I wanted Scott to explain all of these things, especially that business with the cement, and I wanted desperately for him to be convincing. He was my little brother, after all. I didn't want him to be guilty.

• • •

On January 28, Scott appeared on *Good Morning America* with Diane Sawyer. Jackie had told me that Sawyer had been in touch, but she hadn't bothered to tell me that they had met and that she had interviewed Scott. I guess our family ties went only so far. However, to give them the benefit of the doubt, perhaps the Petersons were asked to keep it quiet.

I watched that interview from start to finish, glued to the TV like millions of other people. Scott talked about his "glorious" marriage and about his "amazing" wife, and he said again that he and

Laci had been dealing with his infidelity, which he had told her about and with which she was coming to terms.

"Do you really expect people to believe that an eight-and-a-half-month pregnant woman learns her husband has had an affair and is saintly and casual about it, accommodating, makes a peace with it?" Sawyer asked.

"No one knows our relationship but us," Scott said.

When Sawyer had had enough, she asked him point blank: "I think everybody at home wants the answer to the same question: 'Did you murder your wife?'"

"No," Scott replied. "No. I did not. And I had absolutely nothing to do with her disappearance. And you use the word murder, and right now everyone is looking for a body. And that is the hardest thing because that is not a possible resolution for us. To use the word murder and—yes, and that is a possibility. It's not one we're ready to accept, and it creeps in my mind late at night and early in the morning and during the day all we can think about is the right resolution to find her."

• • •

I called my mother after the interview, knowing that she'd also watched it, but there really wasn't much to say. It didn't look good. Then again, I wasn't calling to analyze his performance. I was calling to see if I could give Scott a key to my parents' cabin in Lake Arrowhead. I was hoping Scott would stop crashing at our home, but—as I had told Tim—I didn't have the heart to leave him in the street.

"That's fine," my mother said, but she wasn't exactly brimming over with enthusiasm. "Whatever you need, honey."

That's family for you. A parent will do anything for her child. And some parents will do too much.

*   *   *

The next time I saw Scott, I didn't even mention the interviews, and he didn't bring them up.

"I spoke to my parents," I said. "They have a little cabin in Lake Arrowhead. I thought you might like to stay there from time to time."

"Why?" he asked. "Don't you want me here?"

"Of course I want you here. You're always welcome here. But it's a nice place, secluded, tucked in the woods, and I thought you might enjoy being on your own from time to time. If nothing else, it'll get you away from the media."

He looked at me like he didn't believe me. He knew exactly what I was saying, and I think he felt betrayed.

"Okay," he said. "Where is it exactly?"

"I'll draw you a map," I said.

My hands were shaking. The Petersons had come into my life in 1997, only five years earlier, and I had been cautious about forging my relationships with them. My brother Don, however, had plunged right in, embracing them from the very start. I'd like to think my circumspect approach was the wiser of the two, but it didn't seem to matter. At the end of the day, the family was falling apart.

"In case your cell doesn't work up there," I said, "I'll call the cabin. I'll let it ring twice then I'll hang up and call back. Okay?"

"Yeah," he said. "Fine."

"Drive carefully."

Scott waved and took off. He was more removed than usual. He knew he was on the verge of losing another ally.

I went into the kitchen, took the empty bottles outside, and dumped them into the recycling bill. It was already full to overflowing. We were consuming way too much alcohol in this house.

"You still think he's innocent?" Tim asked me later that night. We were in bed. I could tell he was mad.

"I'm not sure anymore."

"Well, thank God!" he said sarcastically. "At least we're making progress."

"That was unnecessary."

"What more do you need, Anne? He sits there, watching himself on TV, and he shows no feeling whatsoever. You can't read the guy. Doesn't that spook you?"

"Maybe he's traumatized or in shock or something."

"Jesus. When are you going to stop making excuses for him?"

Scott was back a few nights later, and we were watching the news again, and I was studying him out of the corner of my eye, trying to read him. Suddenly he laughed. I looked over at him. He was grinning a lopsided grin. "This is ridiculous," he said, still grinning.

"What?"

"Every night, it's the same thing. Scott Peterson, Saddam Hussein. Saddam Hussein, Scott Peterson. The two most hated men in the world."

· · ·

Jackie kept calling. "Scott is not an evil person," she said. She kept repeating it over and over again, as if it were her mantra. *Scott is not an evil person.*

Now she was mad at Scott's bosses at Tradecorp. They hadn't exactly fired Scott, but they had asked him to take a little time off, at least until this whole thing blew over. "Scott was very upset," Jackie told me. "He was on his cell phone, screaming at someone from work. I don't know who, but I know I've never seen him so angry in my life."

She told me to hold a minute because another call was coming in and she thought it might be him. When she came back on the line she told me that it was Scott and that he was up in the cabin, at Lake Arrowhead, freezing to death. He had a sleeping bag on the floor in front of the fireplace, and he'd gone out into the bitter cold to gather wood, but he couldn't find much more than a few twigs.

"I'll call him," I said. "I'll take care of it."

I reached him. I let the phone ring twice then called again.

"Scott?"

"Yeah."

"I hear you're freezing?"

"I am."

"Go downstairs. There's a panel on the wall that's hard to see. Slide it back. You'll find an entire cord of wood in there."

"Great. Thanks."

"Call me if you need anything else."

"Okay," he said.

He was still removed, still distant. I guess he was mad at me. If he hadn't been, he would have called me directly. Instead he had used Jackie to enlist my help. Maybe he was trying to tell me that he didn't need me. It was payback time.

But the next afternoon he called me directly. "It's really nice up here," he said.

"I know."

"And it's so peaceful. You were right. I don't have to worry about the press or anyone. From now on, whenever I refer to this place, I'll call it 'Uncle Jim's cabin.'"

"Who's Uncle Jim?" I asked.

"We don't have an Uncle Jim," he said. "That's the point."

I laughed.

"I met one of the neighbors today," Scott said.

"Who?" I was worried he might be recognized.

"It was some little old lady. She was coming home with her groceries, and she was slipping and sliding on the ice, and I went over and helped her."

"Did she say anything?"

He put on an old lady voice: "You're such a nice young man!"

"That's great!"

"I could live up here," he said. "I could be a regular Boy Scout."

. . .

Jackie called the next day, while I was out doing errands, and the babysitter answered.

"Oh, Lorraine," Jackie said, all sweetness. "This is Scott's mom."

"Oh. Hi."

"I wish Scott could meet someone like you."

Lorraine freaked out. She was speechless. When I got home, she repeated the conversation, and I couldn't believe it either. "Are you sure that's what she said?"

"I'm positive. I can't believe she said that to me."

"I don't know," I said. I just couldn't believe it.

I now found myself making excuses for Jackie, just as I'd done for Scott. "This has all been very hard on her. I mean—you know—it's total hell, what she's going through. She's probably a little confused."

Then I wondered what Scott had told his mother about Lorraine. "Mom, you wouldn't believe Anne's sitter! She's a major babe."

The whole thing was insane.

*   *   *

On February 8, a Saturday, 350 people turned out to search for Laci. The search had been organized by Sharon and Ron and their side of the family. I'd never been told about it, of course, since I belonged to the enemy camp. They spent the day walking through pastures and wetlands, in and around Modesto, and to points north, although people were beginning to say that Scott had probably dropped Laci in the San Francisco Bay.

There were two more searches, on two successive Saturdays, but each time there were fewer and fewer people, and when I read the accounts in the local paper I was reduced to tears. People were losing interest, or they were giving up hope.

When I told Scott that the police had again been searching the bay, he sounded petulant. "Why are they wasting their time?" he snapped, his voice getting loud and croaky. "They're such idiots. They're looking in the wrong place."

"Where should they be looking?" I asked.

He immediately changed the subject: "How's my buddy Tim?" he asked with a nasty edge.

That was so unlike him. That was not the Scott I knew. The Scott I knew didn't have a sarcastic bone in his body.

• • •

On February 18, the police went back to Scott's house with another warrant. According to reporters, they spent ten hours looking around. They took his new truck but returned it a few hours later. There were also reports that Laci's sister, Amy, had been escorted into the house by police and that she had remained inside with them for more than an hour.

Scott showed up later that day, which was Ryan's third birthday. I can't remember whether he was driving his truck or a rented car, but I remember exactly what he said as he came through the door. "I was just in Lake Arrowhead. I have a shovel I borrowed that I need to return."

"What?"

"Nothing," he said.

"What shovel?"

"Nothing. A shovel I borrowed."

That was certainly odd. Why was he telling me about a shovel? And what had he been doing with it?

He dropped onto the couch with a stack of mail.

"What's that?" I asked him.

"I just came back from my P.O. box. Is it Ryan's birthday or something?"

I went over to see what he had in his hand. It was a card with a drawing of a birthday cake on the front. There were three little candles in the cake. Scott opened the card. It said, *Happy Birthday Ryan*. There was no name or return address, and I was suddenly very freaked out. Obviously someone knew that Scott was staying with us, and this was his or her way of letting us know.

"Who would send something like that?" I asked. "It's really creepy."

"So it's his birthday today?"

"Yes."

"Who would know it's his birthday?"

"That's what I'd like to know."

Another card had a picture of a praying mantis across the front, which had been cut out of a magazine, but no note. "What an idiot," Scott said. "Everyone knows that mantises eat their lovers, but this moron got it backward. It's the girl that eats the guy."

Then there was a letter in some kind of plastic sheath. There was a childlike, almost cartoon-ish, drawing of Laci, in tears. Beyond it, there was a drawing of Scott and Amber in his truck, with one of those bubble captions over Scott's head: "Come on, baby!"

"The hate mail just keeps on coming," Scott said. He seemed almost amused.

The last envelope contained an actual letter, in an envelope with no return address. Only Scott's name was on it. The letter was written in a clean, feminine hand, in cursive, and I can't remember the exact words, but the message was clear and unmistakable: "We know what you did. You will never be safe. One of us will always be following you. Turn around, we'll be there."

"You should give that to the police," I said.

"Why bother? It's from the Rochas."

"That's ridiculous! How can you say that?"

But I couldn't waste much time worrying about Scott's theories. I was still troubled by the fact that someone knew it was Ryan's third birthday, and that he or she knew that Scott had been staying at our Berkeley home.

· · ·

Scott spent the night again, in the loft, overlooking the bay.

In the morning, I woke up feeling jittery. Whenever a car came down the street, I'd tense up. When the phone rang, I jumped.

"What's wrong with you?" Tim asked me.

"Nothing," I said. "I didn't sleep well."

I felt awful. I wondered if I should have said anything about those cards and letters, but we had enough to deal with already.

Scott came down from the loft at around eight o'clock that morning. He looked unusually glum. At the time, I didn't realize that he'd been on the phone with Amber Frey that morning and that Amber had suggested they stop talking until the case was resolved. I put that together only months later, when I heard those tapes during the trial.

After Tim left for work, Scott parked himself in front of the television and watched police officers moving in and out of his house, hauling off bags and bags of evidence. You could see other officers wandering up and down the driveway with measuring tapes. Scott lost interest. He killed the picture.

"Put it back on," I said. "I think it's almost time for *Murder, She Wrote*." Back then the USA network was running reruns of the show every morning, and they had become a regular part of my morning. I'd get the kids dressed, feed them, then put Tommy into the stroller and walk Ryan to his playschool. When I got back, I would do laundry and try to catch part of the show. It started at ten and again at eleven.

Scott found all this very amusing. He referred to it as my "little routine," and when he was around he became part of it. We'd walk Ryan to school, return home, and watch TV. Sometimes he helped me fold laundry. Other times he played with Tommy.

"So this is your life, eh, Sis?" he asked, laughing. "You take the kids to school. You do laundry. You watch *Murder, She Wrote*."

It *was* my life. I had a three-year-old and a baby and a husband who wasn't all that happy with me at the moment.

• • •

The next day Scott disappeared, and I didn't hear back from him for a couple of days. When he called it was early, and I was watching *Murder, She Wrote*. He said he was almost at my house, and wanted to know if he was missing anything good. I told him it was a great episode, so he should hurry, and asked him if he wanted a BLT sandwich, since I was about to make one for myself.

"Absolutely," he said. "I won't be long."

I found out later that the police were wiretapping the calls, and that was one of the ones they intercepted. I have since wondered what they made of it.

Scott arrived, and we ate our sandwiches in front of the TV. When the show was over, he told me that he and Laci had often spent the night at a bed-and-breakfast in Mendocino that looked a lot like the main house in *Murder, She Wrote.* "One day Laci and I went for a walk, and we ended up in a part of town we'd never seen before. We came across a small cemetery, with an even smaller cemetery just beyond it. The small cemetery was all overgrown with weeds, and the headstones were really small, so we assumed it was a pet cemetery.

"Laci and I climbed over the little broken fence and started to read the headstones. They were really old, and really overgrown, and it was hard to read them. But then we read one and realized that this wasn't a pet cemetery at all. It was a children's cemetery. It was full of little children."

I was holding my breath. The way Scott was telling the story, it seemed almost as if he were in a trance. His voice was flat, hypnotic.

"Laci started crying," he said, continuing in the same, uninflected tone. "She was very upset. She wanted to fix up the place. She wanted to clear out the brush and plant beautiful flowers and make it nice for the children. It was just, you know, it was just really sad."

Scott was staring at me now, and I thought he might be about to cry. I also thought he was trying to tell me something. I had a feeling that the story wasn't true, and that he'd made it up so he could find some way to tell me the truth about everything else.

I could hardly breathe. "What happened?" I asked.

"Nothing," Scott said, and he seemed to snap out of his trance. The spell was broken. "We left the cemetery and went back to town."

He got up and went off to do something on the computer, and I sat there feeling winded and increasingly upset. Maybe Scott hadn't been trying to tell me anything at all; maybe it was my imagination. But that was the moment I knew that Laci and Conner were never coming back.

Scott with his goatee and newly blond hair: February 18, 2003

THE POOL

Scott spent a couple of nights in Lake Arrowhead and returned one afternoon in a foul mood. "I am so sick of all these undercover cops," he said.

"How can you tell they're undercover cops?" I asked.

"Easy," he replied. "I memorize their license plates."

He dropped onto the couch and began flipping through the newspaper, perusing the classifieds. "I think I'd like an apartment in town," he said. "Where would be a good place to look?"

"You could try the Internet," I said.

"I want a roommate," he said. "I'm not going to go through that whole application thing. Who in their right mind would rent to Scott Peterson?"

I didn't say anything, but he had a point. He wandered into the kitchen and poked his nose in the fridge.

"You hungry?" I asked.

He turned to me, lost in thought. "I'm going to change my name. I'm going to start calling myself Cal."

"*Cal?* Where'd you come up with that?"

"That's what Laci and I were going to call the baby. Cal, short for California."

I didn't know what to make of that. All I remembered was that Laci had liked the name Logan, Jackie had objected, and they had eventually agreed on Conner. I couldn't understand why Scott would even say such a thing.

When I left the house later that day, to run errands, I suddenly noticed the profusion of "Cal Berkeley" signs everywhere. The signs refer to the University of California, Berkeley; this is very much a college town. It occurred to me that Scott had pulled his own *Usual Suspects* moment: He just saw the name and went for it.

· · ·

Before long, our phone was ringing off the hook, and most of the calls were for "Cal." All kinds of people, men and women alike, were calling back about the rooms they had for rent. I would take messages for Scott, and Tim would take messages, and before long it got to be a bit much.

"I'm sick of answering the phone for your damn brother. Why couldn't he have given them his cell?"

"I don't know, Tim. I'm sorry."

"I'm sorry, too. What was the point of giving him the key to the cabin if he's going to keep coming back here?"

"Maybe he's lonely."

I looked over at Tim. For a moment there, I could just hear the irresistible response: *Maybe he should have thought of that before he killed his wife and child.* But Tim didn't say that. And he probably wasn't thinking it. It was just me. The pressure was getting to me. My life was unraveling by the minute.

· · ·

Like a bad penny, Scott was back the next day. He had taken the time to answer some of his calls, and there was one apartment that sounded promising. He didn't know the neighborhood, however, so he asked if I'd drive him there to have a look.

As we were crossing the Bay Bridge, I began to have trouble breathing, and Scott was very worried. "What is it?" he asked. "What's wrong?"

It wasn't the first time this had happened. When the police began searching the bay for Laci, I started having trouble driving across bridges—not only the Bay Bridge but also any bridge. By the time they conducted their third search, it had become noticeably worse. Even approaching a bridge filled me with dread, and it was all I could do to make it across.

And the problem kept getting worse. Whenever I left my house, the street took me directly toward the Berkeley Marina, which skirts the edge of the bay. It was getting to the point where just climbing behind the wheel of my car would make me anxious. A few weeks earlier I had talked to my doctor about this, and she had given me a prescription for Xanax, an antianxiety medication.

"I'm okay," I told Scott. "Sometimes I just worry for no reason. I have these little anxiety attacks."

"Anxiety attacks?" Scott repeated, half-smiling, as if he'd never heard the phrase. I guess he wasn't the anxious type.

I kept driving, suddenly wondering why my little orange pills were so erratic, why they worked on some occasions and not on others. I worried that the thought of driving across bridges would fill me with dread for the rest of my life.

I later spoke to my brother Stephen about it—I could confide in him—and he said he thought fear was overrated. "Everyone experiences fear. Anxiety is part of living. Don't worry about it. It's all good."

* * *

A few nights later, I saw Sharon Rocha on the news. She was talking about a very disturbing experience, in which she had imagined seeing Laci on the couch at her home. Laci had smiled and said, "Hi, Mom!" Apparently, she seemed so real that Sharon was tempted to talk to her, but a moment later she disappeared. An expert on the news said that those types of delusions were brought on by either "extreme guilt" or "extreme grief."

When I mentioned the story to Scott, he got a faraway look in his eye. "It's strange you should tell me that," he said. "I've had a couple of similar episodes."

"You saw Laci?"

"Yeah," he said.

"Oh my God. When?"

"Last time was just the other day. I was in the bathroom. I saw her in the mirror."

"Oh my God," I repeated. "What happened? Did she say anything?"

"Just how was I doing and stuff."

"That's all you can remember?" I asked.

"Yes," Scott said, and he turned and headed toward the loft.

The next day, while Scott was out, I called Jackie and told her about it. I repeated what the expert had said about guilt and grief, with the emphasis on guilt.

"What are you saying?" she asked. "Don't be silly! He's innocent and you know he's innocent and before long the whole world will know it."

"Did he ever say anything to you about a shovel he borrowed?" I asked.

"A shovel?"

"Nothing," I said. "Forget it." But the issue of the shovel still troubled me. I don't think it had been particularly snowy in Lake Arrowhead, and the city plows take pretty good care of the roads around my parents' cabin. What had Scott wanted with a shovel? Had he buried something up there? Had anyone even looked?

"You can't honestly look at that boy and tell me you think he had anything to do with this, can you?"

I took a moment. "No, Jackie," I said. "I can't." And I guess I couldn't because I didn't want to. Self-delusion is a wonderful thing.

Jackie called again later that day, and she kept calling. I think she wanted to make sure I was still on her side, and in some ways I believe I fell under her spell. I also felt tremendous sympathy for her. I had two boys of my own, and I knew that I would do anything for them. Well, *almost* anything.

Jackie's situation was much more complicated, however. She'd had four kids: Don, me, John, and Scott. Don and I had gone on to make good lives for ourselves. John had become the family rebel— but a lovable one. And Scott had become the central figure, and a *person of interest,* in the mysterious disappearance of his pregnant wife.

You never know with kids: the ones you give up or the ones you keep.

I wonder if she ever thought about that.

. . .

On March 4, one of the newspapers reported that Lee had complained to the Modesto police about the investigation. He was quoted as saying that the police were so focused on Scott that they were going to blow the case.

The next day, police reclassified the case as a homicide. The lead detective in the case, Craig Grogan, had this to say: "As the investigation has progressed, we have increasingly come to believe that Laci Peterson is the victim of a violent crime."

To me, the timing of the announcement felt deliberate. It was as if police had heard enough criticism from Jackie and Lee and had finally decided to put them in their place.

Jackie herself spoke to the press that same day, and her comments appeared in a number of papers on March 6. She said that reclassifying the case as a homicide would make people stop looking for Laci, and she didn't want them to give up.

. . .

Not long afterward, I heard from Detective Grogan himself. He was calling about the earrings, and I realized that Sharon Rocha must have passed my message along to him. I wondered why it had taken him so long to get back to me, but then I realized that the earrings were the least of it—that they were still looking for Laci and were still hopeful.

Jackie had heard weeks before that he might be contacting me, and she seemed concerned about what I might say to them. "Don't discuss *anything* with the police," she said. She kept repeating this every time we spoke, as if trying to drum it into my head, and I felt a little put out.

"Jackie," I said finally, "that's ridiculous. If the police call me, I'm going to tell them everything I know. Isn't that the point? To be as helpful as possible?"

I could tell she wasn't happy about this. She was already acting as if the police were not on our side.

. . .

Grogan was polite and professional. He asked me about the earrings and then segued into more general questions—about my relationship with Scott, with Laci, with Jackie, and with the rest of the family. I told him some of the history: how I'd reconnected with my biological family and how much I'd come to like them, especially Scott and Laci. I told him I thought Scott was not only a nice guy, but also a good person.

"There is no chance he did this," I said.

He asked me about Amber, and whether I had known about her. He wondered if I knew about any other affairs. I was honest about this, too. I told him what Scott had told me about that fling with the girl in San Luis Obispo. I didn't say anything about the women on the plane because I just wasn't sure whether I believed that story.

"This girl in San Luis Obispo, did he give you a name?"

"No," I said. "No name."

After I hung up, I realized that the authorities already knew a great deal about me. Most pointedly, they knew that Scott had been staying at our home. I began to wonder whether this whole case would end badly, and what role I might be called upon to play. If, God forbid, Scott was somehow implicated in Laci's disappearance—and I really didn't want to think about that—would I be called upon to testify? And who would I be testifying for: the prosecution or the defense?

Many months later, when the trial finally got under way, my name came up only once. Detective Grogan was being questioned by Mark Geragos, who had replaced Kirk McAllister as Scott's attorney. Geragos asked Detective Grogan about his conversation with me. But the question was phrased in that sneaky lawyer way, so that Geragos could make the only point he wanted make. He simply asked Grogan whether I had indeed told him there was "no chance" Scott had committed this crime, and Grogan's only option was to give him a one-word answer: "Yes."

To this day, people assume that Scott's sister continues to believe her brother is innocent. They assume wrong. By the time they reach the end of this book, my feelings should be perfectly clear.

*   *   *

I told Scott about my talk with Detective Grogan. I didn't see any reason not to. He was curious about the questions he had asked me, and I told him they were pretty standard questions: the earrings, family stuff, and our relationship.

A few nights later, Scott went out with a relative from Jackie's side of the family, one of the ones I'd met at the family reunion—the one everyone had identified as gay. He and some friends took Scott to a gay bar, and Scott drank too much and made a fool of himself. That was the report I got: that he'd been loud and boisterous and eager for attention.

When Scott crawled out of bed the following morning, nursing a hangover, he told me the night was a bust. "No one hit on me," he said.

I laughed. I thought he was kidding around. But he hadn't been kidding around. When I spoke to another relative later, she confirmed it. "Scott was pretty bummed," she said. "He thought for sure everyone would want to hit on a stud like him. But no one did."

When my next phone bill arrived, I found all sorts of mysterious calls to two numbers in Fresno. I figured the calls were to Amber Frey, but I didn't say anything to Scott. I didn't see any point in questioning him. Besides, right about the time I discovered the two numbers on my phone bill, he came home sporting a bad dye job, and that was certainly more interesting than my phone bill. His hair had gone a sort of dusty, brownish-blond, with a hint of orange in it. I'd made similar mistakes in my own youth.

"What happened to your hair?" I asked. "Did you dye it?"

"No," he replied. "I was up at Mammoth, skiing with some friends, and I think there was too much chlorine in the hotel swimming pool. It bleached it out."

Scott had gone to Mammoth on a ski trip with his friends? It could be true, but that was the first I'd heard of it. And I'd never heard of a swimming pool turning someone's hair blond. *Green*, yes—but not blond.

Even the goatee was badly bleached.

• • •

It was during this period that Scott began to obsess about the swimming pool at his house. He drove home to clean it out and to mow the lawn, and two weeks later he went back to do it again. When he told me he was going back for a third time, I thought it was getting a little bizarre, so I finally confronted him. "What's the big deal with the pool?"

"Nothing. It gets dirty. You don't clean it, it turns green."

"So what? Nobody's using it."

"I don't want the neighbors to see it."

I'd never been to his house, so I didn't know whether the pool was visible from next door, but that wasn't the issue anymore. I couldn't help thinking about what Laci had told me about the pool, and how she'd slip into the water to take the pressure off her aching back. I pictured her floating in the water, her hands resting on her big belly.

Much later I would find myself wondering whether Scott had drowned Laci in the pool, which would have been effortless and soundless and would have left no evidence of a struggle. From there he could have put her body into the back of the truck, covered her with the tarp, and driven her to the Berkeley Marina the next day. It's just a theory, and for all I know it's already been looked into and dismissed. Maybe there would have been chlorine in her system, although after all those months in the ocean, would it have been possible to tell? I don't know. I'm not an expert. All I know is that Scott kept obsessing over that swimming pool and that later I had night-mares about what might have happened there.

I didn't say a word, of course. But I was worried. Scott was acting increasingly bizarre, and his behavior was beginning to frighten me.

Sometimes he looked like a man without a care in the world, and this only fueled my fears. There seemed to be a huge disconnect between Scott and the world around him. I got the impression that he was waiting for this whole thing to blow over so he could get on with his life.

· · ·

March 21 is Tim's birthday. We really hadn't planned much because we weren't feeling particularly festive. Lorraine, the babysitter, was there, helping with the kids, but neither of us felt like going out. These last months had been really trying, particularly with Scott still insisting on hanging around the house, and the rift between Tim and me was only getting larger.

The phone rang, and it was Scott. "Hey," he said. "It's me. Isn't it Tim's birthday today? What are you guys doing to celebrate?"

"I don't know," I said. "Nothing yet. We're here with Lorraine, trying to figure it out."

"I'll be right over!" Scott said.

Well, I thought. *That was certainly subtle.*

Scott arrived with a bottle of peach schnapps, and the moment he came through the door he had eyes only for Lorraine. He told us he was going to make a round of drinks called "flirtinis"—apparently, he had heard about them on *Sex and the City*—and he got to work on them right away. They were terrible. Tim and I went back to wine, but Lorraine didn't want to insult Scott, so she played along. At first, she seemed to be having fun, but after the second drink she became self-conscious. She told me that this whole thing was too much for her, wished Tim a happy birthday, and left.

"Your brother's a hottie," she said as she was leaving, when we were out of earshot. "But my God." Scott was coming on a little too strong. "My boyfriend's waiting for me at home."

The evening was very strange. We ate some leftovers, Scott crashed in the loft, and Tim and I went to bed, both of us feeling depressed.

• • •

In the morning, Jackie called. "How was Tim's birthday?" she asked.

"Could have been better."

"Scott called me yesterday when he was on his way over. He said your sitter was there. He told me a while ago that she's really cute."

"She *is* cute," I said. "She's also twenty-two years old and has a boyfriend."

Jackie sighed. "I wish Scott would meet someone like Lorraine," she said.

"What?" I had heard this from Lorraine: I hadn't believed it then, and I couldn't believe it now. "What did you just say?"

"When you see Scott, have him call me, will you?"

It sounded like Jackie was becoming unhinged.

• • •

In early April, I decided to go visit my parents in San Diego, and Scott said he wanted to come along.

"I usually leave at 4:00 A.M.," I said. "To avoid traffic."

"Four A.M. it is."

I was up by 3:00 A.M., getting organized, and Scott impressed me by appearing in the kitchen under his own steam. He watched me get ready for the trip—blankies, stuffed toys, snacks to be doled out at various points along the drive—and he started laughing. "Look at you go!" he said. "You're funny!"

I guess I can get pretty frenetic about travel, but it works for me.

I went into the bedroom, kissed my sleeping husband good-bye, and off we went. Scott said he might stop in on the way and look in on his parents, then promptly fell asleep.

The boys fell asleep too, and about three hours into the drive I desperately had to go to the bathroom. I pulled into a gas station and left them in the car, with the key still in the ignition, and went off to use the facilities. As I was washing my hands, it occurred to me that I had left Scott alone with my two kids. Then I tried to put the thought out of my head. It was not only silly, but also unfair. There wasn't the slightest possibility that he would hurt my children. Still, it bothered me, and I hurried back to the car, only to find that all three of them were still fast asleep. As I climbed behind the wheel, I checked to make sure I'd brought my antianxiety medication. I had. Just knowing it was there made me feel better instantly.

When Scott woke up, he did so with a start. It was pouring out, and we were squeezed in the center lane between two gigantic big rigs, and he just sat there frozen and tense until the trucks had passed.

"That was really something to wake up to," he said.

"I thought maybe you were having a bad dream," I said.

"I never have bad dreams."

When he was fully awake, he offered to take over, and I let him drive. He was an excellent driver: cautious and courteous. He'd also been up and down this stretch of interstate many times, and he was familiar with the area farms. "Those are Brussels sprouts," he said at one point. At another, he pointed out the almonds.

Later on, we passed a sign that read, *Where Water Flows, Food Grows*, and Scott started talking about farming, irrigation, and the shortage of water in the Central Valley. I remember being very impressed by the depth of his knowledge.

By late morning, the sun was out, and by early afternoon we arrived in San Diego.

• • •

This was the first time my parents had seen Scott since Laci's disappearance, and they were very attentive. They told him how sorry they were about Laci and about what he was going through, and they said they hoped everything would come out for the best. Scott's eyes welled up with tears, and my mother was in tears herself. "Thank God for family," my mother said. "You kids should do your best to relax and go out and have a good time and not think about any of this."

My father didn't say much because that isn't his style, but I had a sense there was a lot going on inside. I know now that he wasn't comfortable with Scott in the house, but he had enough respect for me, and for my feelings, to keep his thoughts to himself.

I took Scott to the Brigantine, a neighborhood restaurant that's right next to the San Diego Yacht Club. It's in Point Loma, and I know a lot of people there; the moment we walked in I saw three or four familiar faces. We had a round of drinks with my friends, and I introduced them to "my brother Scott." I didn't use his last name, but I didn't have to: Everyone knew who he was, and one of my friends actually tried to ask him some questions. Scott made it clear, gently, that he wasn't in the mood. From that point on, everyone acted like he was just a regular guy and not someone who was slowly becoming the prime suspect in an ongoing murder investigation.

After that first drink, a group of us had another quick drink at the Bali Hai, a Polynesian bar, and ended up at the Ballast, a neighborhood pub. We played a little pool and ordered another round of drinks.

I realize now that there was a lot of drinking going on that night. But then that was the idea: to get a break from all of this, to stop thinking for a night or two.

At one point, when Scott went up to the bar to buy a round, he pulled a huge wad of Mexican pesos from his pocket. One of my friends, whom I'll call Gordo, was a little taken aback, and he asked Scott if he was planning a trip to Mexico in the near future. Scott ignored the question, paid for the drinks in dollars, and rejoined us.

A few minutes later, Gordo called me aside. He was a little drunk, but then again, so was I. "What?" I asked.

"You know, Annie,"—he always called me Annie—"I really like you, and I don't want you to disappear."

"What's that supposed to mean?"

"Nothing," he said. He didn't tell me about the pesos until later that evening, when we were all back at his house.

I had another friend there, whom I'll call Charlie. He was also adopted, by a well-to-do family. He drives a Ferrari. When we went outside, to continue the party at Gordo's house, Scott saw the Ferrari and was very impressed. He immediately buddied up to Charlie, which Charlie found pretty amusing, and wanted to ride with him. But I already had dibs on the Ferrari, and Scott ended up in Gordo's car.

On the way to Gordo's house, Gordo turned to Scott and asked him, "Did you kill your wife?" The minute the words were out of his mouth, he realized he shouldn't have asked, but he had been drinking heavily. . . . He shouldn't have been behind the wheel of a car, either.

"No," Scott said. "I loved my wife."

Gordo told me about this back at his house, where he also told me about the Mexican money. "He used 'loved.' Past tense. Does that tell you anything?"

"No," I said. It didn't tell me anything because I'd had too much to drink, and the reason I'd had too much to drink is because I was tired of hearing about this. I was in San Diego to get away from all the madness, but the madness followed me wherever I went.

Just then, Scott asked Gordo if he could use his computer. "I need to look something up," he said.

"What?" Gordo asked. He was openly hostile to Scott, but Scott had drank plenty himself, so I'm not sure he even noticed.

"I want to see if the cops have released my passport," he said. "They're supposed to release my passport."

I didn't know they'd taken his passport.

"Sure," Gordo said, and Scott disappeared down the hallway. Gordo turned to me. "That is a total crock of shit. How can he check something like that on the Web? What does he think—the cops have created a link to his passport?"

"He's probably just curious about what was on the news today," I said. "We've been on the road. He hasn't seen a newspaper or watched the news. And he likes going to Laci's website, to read the letters and stuff."

Gordo shook his head and looked at me like I was crazy. I guess he was concerned about me. He was trying to be a good friend.

• • •

We didn't get back to my parents' house till two in the morning, and my mother was a little annoyed. It was clear she'd been worried, although she didn't say so.

In the morning, nursing a pretty bad hangover, I went over to see my friend Amy and her mom, Buffy. Scott came with me. Amy thought she recognized him, but she wasn't sure, so she asked him what he did for a living. He said he was a man of leisure. "My wife and I spend most of our time at the country club, swimming," he noted. He also said he had a terrible hangover, so Buffy made him a screwdriver.

From there, we went to Rancho's for breakfast. We had arranged to meet Jackie, along with Jackie's brother Patrick and Scott's brother John, and his wife, Alison. I hadn't seen John and Alison since our trip to Disneyland. My mother came, too. Unfortunately, the event was short-lived. Before the food arrived, I was sick to my stomach. I'd like to lie and say it was a bug, but it was the alcohol.

I went home to recover, and my Mom took Ryan to the San Diego Zoo for one of their "special days." Although my mother's name is Jerri, he calls her Gigi. At one point, they were standing in front of the koala bear exhibit and Ryan turned to her out of the blue and said, "Gigi, did you know we can't find Aunt Laci?"

My mother was taken aback, but she handled it. "Don't worry, sweetheart. We'll find her. Everything's going to be all right."

That night, my friend Charlie invited Scott and me to join his wife and a few other friends for dinner at the San Diego Yacht Club. He was clearly intrigued by Scott. We ended up taking little Tommy with us because he was fussing and I didn't want to saddle my mother with both boys two nights in a row. I had also promised her it would be an early night.

When we got to the Yacht Club, I introduced Scott to Charlie's wife, who was as intrigued by Scott as her husband. I noticed that people recognized Scott, but if it bothered him he didn't let it show.

At one point, in the middle of our meal, Charlie turned to me and said I was a very lucky girl.

"How so?" I asked.

"I wish I had what you had," he said.

"In what sense?"

He indicated Scott. "To have a brother like that. To have someone you're so close to."

Knowing what he knew about the ongoing investigation, I thought that was a little strange. But I also thought it was very generous: Unlike the rest of the country, he was giving Scott the benefit of the doubt.

I had told everyone, including Scott, that we had to make this an early night, so after a quick dinner we went over to the Bali Hai for a nightcap. At one point, with Tommy fussing in my lap, I turned to Scott and reminded him, pointedly, that we had to be back by nine.

"Who cares?" he asked.

That took me by surprise. He said it in a really nasty way, and then he got up and went to the bar and ordered a bunch of drinks for the table. They were those big, foamy, tropical concoctions, and I was getting irritated. But neither Charlie nor his wife seemed irritated, and their friends seemed pretty mellow, too, so I had a drink and tried to chill out.

After another round of drinks, I reminded Scott for the third time that we had to get going.

"Who cares about your nine o'clock curfew?" he snapped. "No one cares. *Okay*?"

To say that his comment was off-putting is putting it mildly. I had never seen that side of Scott, and it was hurtful. I knew he was under a lot of stress, but I couldn't understand why he had to treat me so shabbily. For almost four months now, ever since Laci's disappearance, I had been among his staunchest allies. This behavior was unacceptable.

I kept wondering if something else was going on, and I noticed that he still seemed intent on cementing his new friendship with my friend Charlie. I wondered what that was about.

*   *   *

We didn't get back to my parents' place till 10:30 P.M., but Ryan was happily asleep, and my mother was less nervous than she'd been the previous evening.

In the morning, we headed back to Berkeley. Scott and I didn't say much en route. I think he was still a little mad at me, although I'm the one who should have been mad.

Shortly after we arrived, he showered and changed his clothes and told me he was taking off. He looked refreshed and handsome—the old Scott, the perfect, wholesome, all-American boy. He didn't say where he was going, but I had a feeling he wanted to crash at the cabin in Lake Arrowhead.

On April 13, a tiny body was found in San Francisco Bay. Police were working on identifying it, but I told myself it couldn't possibly be Conner.

The next day, they found the body of a woman.

I couldn't keep it inside anymore. The minute I found out—it was around ten in the morning—I reached Scott on his cell. "Did you hear?" I asked. "They found the body of a woman in the bay."

"It's not Laci," he said with an edge. I could almost picture the sneer of disgust on his face. "They'll find out it's not Laci, and they'll just keep looking."

"But they found a baby yesterday," I said.

"What?!" he asked, his voice rising in anger. "Who would do such a thing? That's terrible! Who would do such a thing?!"

"Where are you?" I asked.

"About forty-five minutes from your place," he said.

"I'm going to watch the news now," I said.

"Okay," he said. And he hung up.

I turned on the news. They were showing clips of the places

where the bodies had been found and waiting for word from the police.

The whole thing was happening two miles from my house.

By the time Tim came home, I was a wreck. "Did you hear?" I asked.

"Yes," he said.

"I'm freaking out," I said.

"That makes two of us."

We sat down in front of the TV, glued to the news. Every reporter on every channel was asking the same question: *Where is Scott Peterson?*

We didn't know either.

At the county jail in Modesto after his arrest: April 18, 2003

CHAPTER

VII

THE
ARREST

It would be forty-eight hours before the police confirmed that the two bodies recovered from the San Francisco Bay were indeed those of Laci Peterson and her unborn son, Conner. But everyone had already assumed the obvious.

Shortly after I spoke to Scott, when I had told him about the second body, I tried to contact him again. I called the cabin in Lake Arrowhead, let the phone ring twice, then hung up and redialed. There was no answer.

I called Jackie. She sounded flat, not at all like herself, and she told me she had no idea where he was. She sounded evasive, too, almost cold, but I think she was simply in shock.

She said almost exactly what Scott had said—"It's not them"— and told me not to worry.

Then I called my doctor, Dr. Toni Brayer of Cal Pacific Medical Center, and I told her that I needed to talk to someone before I went into shock myself. She called me back a few minutes later with the name of a therapist, who came highly recommended. I placed a call to Dr. Linda Tucker, and she called me back right away. I told her I was Scott Peterson's sister and that I was falling apart, and she made room for me that very afternoon.

I liked her the minute I walked into her office. I sat down and gave her a very short version of my life story, with the emphasis on recent events. I spoke about my relationship with Scott, with Jackie, and with my own parents; I told her about Tim and about our crumbling marriage; and I told her about my two little boys and how badly I wanted to be the World's Most Perfect Mother. I was trying to be as honest as possible, even if it made me look bad, because I knew too many people who lied to their therapists, and they never seemed to get better.

"I can see you have a lot on your plate," Dr. Tucker said. "Let's try to get you feeling a bit more stabilized, and we'll tackle these problems together, one at a time."

I went to see Dr. Tucker again the next day and the day after that.

"Everybody's looking for Scott." I said. "Everybody wants to know where he is. I can't understand why he didn't go directly to the police station to do what he could to identify his wife and child."

Dr. Tucker didn't say anything, but her gentle eyes said enough: *When are you going to wake up, Anne?*

"Do you think Scott is guilty?" I asked her.

"How could I know such a thing?" she replied. "I only know what it is that you've told me, and up until now you have not wanted to believe that he could have done such a thing."

"Yes, but you see it on the news," I said, pushing for an answer. "You must have an opinion as to his guilt or innocence."

"Anne," she said. "I'm not trying to evade your question. What really is most important is what you think, and I know how difficult an answer this might be for you."

"I don't know what I think anymore," I said. "It's just, you know—those don't seem like the actions of someone who cares."

I still couldn't accept even the *possibility* that Scott was guilty. In the weeks to come, Dr. Tucker would help me through a great deal. But for the moment I remained shrouded in a fog of self-delusion.

Shortly after I got home, I remembered that my parents were leaving for London that afternoon, and I thought I might have missed them. I called the house and saw that it was after five. I realized they were already en route to the airport, so I hung up after two rings.

Then I had a strange thought, and I dialed the number again.

"Hello?"

It was him.

"Scott?"

"How did you know I was here?"

"I didn't. I just guessed. What are you doing there?"

I'd given him a key to their house when we'd gone down to visit, but I couldn't believe he was there—now, of all times. I didn't say anything, but I felt as if he had violated my trust.

"I don't know. I was just driving, and I found myself near San Diego, and I came here."

"Why didn't you go to Lake Arrowhead?"

"I started to, but the roads were slippery and the car spun out."

He was lying. I could just tell. Plus, the numbers didn't add up. I believe he was either around Berkeley or Modesto when I'd last talked to him—he'd said he was forty-five minutes from my place—so to reach San Diego so quickly he would have had to find the nearest freeway and bolted south. I remembered what Gordo had told me about that wad of Mexican pesos, and I immediately thought that he was headed for Mexico. Maybe I was wrong. Maybe he wasn't going to Mexico. Or maybe he was and changed his mind because he figured they'd be watching the border.

I wanted to ask him, but I didn't have the guts. "What are you going to do?" I asked instead.

"I don't know," he said. "I'm going to rest."

That very evening, not an hour later, Natalie, a friend of my sister's, arrived at the house where Scott had made himself at home. She was supposed to be taking care of the place while my parents were away, and she had stopped in to turn on a few lights. As soon as she walked through the door, she almost jumped out of her skin. Scott was parked in front of one of the computers, a bottle of wine at his side.

"Hey," he said, turning to look at her. "Who are you?"

For a few moments, Natalie couldn't say anything. She knew who he was. She knew about his connection to me and to my family, and only minutes earlier she had been watching the news on TV. There was little else on TV that day, at least up and down the coast of California. Two bodies had been recovered in the San Francisco Bay, and everyone was waiting for word from the police.

"I'm Natalie," she said when she found her voice. "I'm taking care of the house while the Gradys are overseas."

"Oh," Scott said.

"What are you doing?" she asked.

"My taxes. It's April 14, right? Tomorrow is tax day."

"You're right," she said.

He stood up and moved very close to her. "Would you like a glass of wine?"

He was practically in her face; she backed up, flustered, and tried to turn it into a little joke. "You're one of those close talkers," she said.

"So what are you supposed to do here?" Scott asked, ignoring the remark. "What's there to take care of?"

"Not that much. Pick up the mail and stuff. I used to feed the cat, but the cat died."

"Did you kill the cat?" he asked.

"No," she said, and she decided it was time to leave. "Are you going to be staying here a while?"

"I don't know," Scott said. "Why?"

"Maybe you could bring in the mail."

"Why don't you give me your phone number, Natalie?"

"Excuse me?"

"That way I'll call you and let you know when I'm leaving, so you can take care of the mail."

Natalie gave Scott her number—the police found it in his pocket three days later, when they arrested him—and hurried off.

After Natalie called me to tell me about her bizarre encounter with Scott, I phoned Jackie. She was coming out of her slump—but her depression was giving way to anger. "Everyone is so wrong about him," she said. "Scott is not an evil person. Only an evil person would do something like this. You know Scott, Anne. You know how sweet he is. You know he could never do something like this."

"It's terrible," I said, looking for a noncommittal answer, and she launched right back into her litany of complaints: The Rochas were determined to frame her son, the police had never thoroughly investigated the most promising leads, and the media were just looking to boost their ratings.

When she was done, I tried to get back on track. "Jackie, I'm really worried. It's a woman and a baby." We were still waiting for the bodies to be positively identified.

"It's not them," she said.

"How can you say that?"

"Because it's not! It's not Laci and Conner. What we have to do is think about Scott. We have to protect Scott."

I felt as if Jackie was being destroyed by anguish. My heart was breaking for her.

I remembered the day of Tommy's christening and the way Lee had turned to the priest for advice. "What is someone to do in a situation like this? . . . How does one get through it?"

Now I understood what he had meant. He was talking about survival.

*   *   *

The next day, my brother Michael went over to our parents' house to do his laundry. He walked into the kitchen and found Scott sitting there, watching himself on TV.

"Who are you?" Scott asked.

"I'm Anne's brother Michael," he said.

"Michael. Of course. I've heard a lot about you." He stood up and shook Michael's hand. "I'm Anne's brother, too."

They had met, briefly, at my wedding, but only in passing, and I'm not sure they were ever formally introduced.

"So you're going to do your laundry?"

"Yeah," Michael said. "I'll just put it in and leave."

"Don't hurry off on my account," Scott said.

Michael called me from his cell as he was pulling out of the driveway. "What is going on? What is he doing there, in our parents' house? Everyone's looking for him. We need to tell the police."

"The police aren't looking for him," I said. "*Reporters* are looking for him."

"I don't like this," Michael said. "I don't like this at all."

• • •

On April 18, police announced that they had used DNA samples to positively identify the bodies of Laci and Conner.

When I heard the news, I remember I began to sob uncontrollably; when Ryan came home from day care I was still a complete wreck. I tried to hide it from him, but he knew something was terribly wrong. Still, I wasn't prepared for what he said. "Is this about Laci?"

"Yes," I said.

Somehow, his three-year-old mind was aware that she wasn't coming back. He went into his room, grabbed the old crib mattress that we keep under his bed, and began pulling it toward the front door.

"What are you doing, honey?" I asked him.

"I'm taking this outside for when Laci falls down from the heavens."

It was all I could do to not burst into tears all over again. Only a few days earlier, he had been asking me about death, which is not atypical for children at his age. He wanted to know what happened to people when they died, and I told him that they went up to the heavens.

"And then God fixes them, and they come back, right?" he had asked me.

"That's right, Ryan," I had said. "God fixes them."

. . .

Later that very day, Scott was arrested in the parking lot of the Torrey Pines Municipal Golf Course, near San Diego. He was carrying fifteen thousand dollars in cash.

Among the items found in his car were several knives, including a double-edged dagger with a T-handle, a folding saw, duct tape, climbing equipment and rope, and a Mapquest map downloaded that day with directions to American Bodyworks, where Amber Frey was employed.

It was over. My brother had reached the end of the road.

Three days later, on April 23, Scott was brought into the Stanislaus County Superior Court and charged with two felony counts of murder. He pled not guilty.

. . .

For several days after Scott's arrest, I couldn't get over the fact that Laci's body had been dumped in the San Francisco Bay, practically in my front yard. I had invited Scott into our home, given him safe haven, as it were. And the room I had given him overlooked Laci's watery grave.

I don't know how he slept at night.

Jackie called within hours of the arrest, and she was beside herself. She began talking about things I'd been catching snippets of on the news—the Mercedes-Benz he was driving, the large amount of cash—as if she were already plotting out his defense.

The Mercedes-Benz was hers, she told me. She had asked Scott to buy the car for *her*. And the fifteen thousand dollars in cash was to be used for his legal defense.

When I got off the phone, I called Dr. Tucker and told her I needed to talk to her. She made room for me that same afternoon, and in the months ahead I began seeing her two and three times a week.

The problem was really quite simple: I still refused to accept the possibility that Scott was guilty. Dr. Tucker's job, as I saw it, was to help me remove my rose-colored glasses. Until I was finally able to separate fact from fiction, I wouldn't find my way back. She was eager to help me find my way, but she never forced it: She wanted me to get there on my own.

"But why do *you* assume he's guilty?" I asked her again.

"I don't assume he's guilty," she replied. "How could I possibly know? All I know is what you tell me, and everything you've told me indicates that you don't want to believe he did this. Now it looks like the doubts are taking hold, and I can see it frightens you."

"It does," I said. "I was very close to him. I was very close to Laci."

"I know," she said.

"I told my son all about his little cousin."

"You know, Anne," she said gently, "you have told me many things about Scott, including that you always seem to be making excuses for him. You have also told me many things that don't seem to add up as you have explained them. I know how hard this is because you do love Scott, and because you want to help him in any way you can. But it's not going to help you or anyone else if you refuse to see things for what they are."

Later that day, I was in a neighborhood grocery store with both my kids when I noticed the two women in line behind me, poring over the *National Enquirer*. They were looking at an article about Scott.

"I can't believe that monster killed his wife and baby," one of them said. "He makes me sick."

The second woman nodded in agreement. "He should be put straight to death," she suggested. "They should just skip the trial."

I was absolutely numb. It was all I could do to get my kids, and my groceries, back to the car.

• • •

Less than ten days after Scott's arrest, I got a letter from him. It was written in pencil, from his cell at the Stanislaus County Jail, in Modesto, where he was taken right after his arrest. "I actually had a dream that I was waking up in your loft with a little breeze through the window," he wrote. "It was better than really being there though because Laci and Conner were in my dream as well. We were all sharing the morning together. I was told that they were gone on the car ride back to Modesto by the detectives. I didn't believe them, wouldn't believe them . . ."

He also discussed his legal defense, noting that Jackie and Lee had talked to attorney Mark Geragos about taking his case. "I was going to go with the public defender because of cost," he wrote. "Now Mom and my Dad have struck a deal with a prominent defender and I don't know if I should accept it because they will sacrifice their financial future to get a job done that a public defender could probably do."

On April 30, I wrote back.

Dear Scott,

I have been at a loss for words when it comes to your loss of Laci and Conner. I am just so sad and heartbroken and it must be so terrible for you.

Do you remember at Tommy's christening, what the rector said? "They're in God's hands." I am sure they are there, and know how much they mean to all of us. Especially to you.

I think about you all the time and wish that this pain and anguish would go away. I wish there were something more I could do to help. Please let me know if there is anything at all.

It is OK for you to break down and cry. I think it's just expected. This is horrendous for you to deal with. We all love you so much and wish we could take the pain away.

God bless you, Laci and baby Conner.

We love you, Anne, Tim, Ryan and Tommy

He wrote back to thank me for my support and kind thoughts, and I replied immediately.

Dear Scott,

I just love your letters, they are so sweet and you have so much compassion and kindness. I don't know how you do it.

Today I went to the mail and a letter I wrote to you came back. It said "no cards."

I'll switch to only stationery from now on . . .

Congratulations on Mark Geragos. I am so happy. I am sure he will do a great job.

I sent you *Islands* and *Traveler* magazine subscriptions so you can read up . . .

I love that you're doing yoga. Good for you! Who sent you that book?

Yes, I am keeping up with Jessica Fletcher. I keep thinking about how you and Laci stayed there, were you both fans of the show?

I'm going to write more tomorrow—the kids aren't quite in bed yet.

But I soon returned to finish the letter.

Scooby-Doo is entertaining the little guys for a few minutes. It's been pouring rain for two days now so we're stuck inside. It's supposed to let up tomorrow.

We put down green Astroturf in the deck of 'your room.' Did I tell you already? I bought some children's chairs, table, umbrella and a Buzz Lightyear swimming pool. Ryan loves it, and Tommy's playpen is out there now. It's nice to have a little outdoor area for them—although it is soaking wet up there now! It took me so long to blow up the pool. I'll have to take a picture of it all so you can have a good laugh.

Keep sending your letters for me to forward. I'll copy all—file in a binder and forward them on while you're away at camp.

Love, Anne

I hadn't been able to bring myself to write the word "jail," so I used the word "camp" instead. I know it seems silly but that was how I felt.

That same week, the first week of May, Geragos announced publicly that he had been hired by Scott's family and would be replacing the team of public defenders who had been assigned to him. "Scott looks forward to finding out who did this," he said.

Also in May, the newspapers reported that Sharon Rocha and her family had gone into Scott and Laci's house and taken a few things, including the baby's crib. I thought maybe Sharon needed a little something to hold onto, and my heart went out to her. But the story didn't end there. People were saying that Laci's family had been forced to break in because the locks had been changed, and Jackie had refused to give them the key or the code to the alarm.

"That's not true!" Jackie said. "I gave them the key and the code."

"It doesn't matter now," I said. "It's done."

"But we paid for that crib! We paid for that crib!"

I didn't see how that mattered. If Sharon Rocha took solace from having the crib near her, why couldn't Jackie let it go? It dawned on me that the crib was the least of it. Jackie seemed to need something to get angry about. It must have kept her from going to a deeper, darker place.

Months later, when the Rochas went back for some more of Laci's belongings, Jackie said she was worried because Scott had something in the house that "really mattered to him and that he would like them for when he is released."

"What things?" I asked.

"His wine collection and his humidor," she replied.

I didn't understand how she could even be thinking about such things.

• • •

Ironically, the next time I spoke to Jackie it was my turn to talk about material goods. One of the local newspapers reported that Scott had given Amber some jewelry, and it made me think of the sapphire cocktail ring I'd wanted Jackie to sell for me, the one that turned up on Laci's hand at her baby shower.

"That wasn't your ring," Jackie said.

"I'm pretty sure it was," I said. It felt incredibly petty, but I couldn't help myself. I wanted to know.

"All those cocktail rings from the sixties look alike," she said.

Then she thought about it for a moment and corrected herself. She suddenly remembered that she had bought the ring herself, to give to a friend as a gift. "Didn't I send you a check?" she asked.

"No," I said. "I never got a check from you."

"Are you sure?"

"I'm positive."

I couldn't believe we were having this conversation. Scott was in jail, and we were talking about a silly ring.

When we spoke the next day, the ring was still on her mind. "Scott told me that you gave that ring to Laci," she said.

At that point I just dropped it. I didn't care about the ring; I just wanted to make sure that Scott hadn't given it to Amber. This business with the ring was getting as convoluted and confusing as the many conflicting stories about the fifteen thousand dollars the police found on Scott at the time of his arrest. Initially, Jackie had told me that the money was for his legal defense, but now she said that Scott had simply been in the process of transferring cash from one bank to another. By week's end, I heard two more versions. The first was pretty half-hearted: "Scott always carries a lot of cash." The second was kind of mystifying: "I sold my membership at the club in Solana Beach and for some reason they gave me cash instead of a check, and Scott was en route to the bank to deposit the money." It was all getting too hard to follow or believe.

*   *   *

Scott continued to write from jail. The food was hideous. He was next to the drunk tank, and the noise was driving him crazy. It was hard for him to keep track of the days, he wrote. But he seemed to be taking solace in his memories: "The trip to San Diego with you was fun," he wrote. "I'm lucky to have such a bighearted sister."

Meanwhile, Jackie kept calling, sometimes two and three times a day. She always complained about the media, noting that their stories were invariably wrong. But I couldn't help noticing that *her* stories were pretty contradictory, too.

I never asked Jackie any questions. *She* asked all the questions, and she gave the answers, too. Why did Scott have a water purifier in his car when he was arrested? Not because he was racing for the Mexican border, but because—"as you know, Anne"—he liked very clean water. Why was he carrying his brother John's ID? Because the police had taken *his* ID. Why did he have so many clothes in his car? Because he didn't have a home anymore.

It was almost as if she were trying to determine whether her reasons were viable, and she must have thought I would be a useful sounding board.

It broke my heart. She was my biological mother. We had found each other and grown close over the years. We had vacationed together, laughed together, and enriched each other's lives in the truest sense of the word.

Now her son had been arrested for murder, and she was desperate. She would go to any lengths to save him, do anything for her little boy, fight to the death if she had to.

I wanted to help her, but I didn't know where to begin. I was pretty traumatized myself. So I listened. And part of me continued to believe.

Tim was less understanding. Now that Scott was finally out of the house, Jackie was calling at all hours, and he was sick of it.

"What are you?" he asked. "Her therapist?"

"I'm her friend."

"Why you? She's got two other kids. She's got a husband. He's got kids of his own. Why doesn't she call someone else for a change?"

"I guess it's because we were close and because I felt so close to Scott."

The calls continued, and Tim decided to do something about it. He sat down with a friend at work and told him all about "flirtini" night. The way Scott had shown up with that bottle of schnapps; the way he was practically drooling over Lorraine, our babysitter; and the fact that Lorraine became so uncomfortable with the attention that she left early.

The story appeared in the *National Enquirer*, as Tim knew it would. They got most of it right, which was good enough for Tim. The whole idea was to drive a wedge between Jackie and me. She would know the story had come from our house.

It almost worked.

"Was that Tim's doing?" Jackie called to ask, furious. "Was it?!"

"Probably, Jackie. What can I say?"

"Where else would they get the story? Certainly not from Lorraine."

"You're right."

"I want you to tell Tim that he's a drunk, and that if they ever put him on the stand he would not make a very credible witness."

That hurt. Tim was not a drunk. We had all been drinking a lot, yes, but that had been precipitated by Scott's presence in our home. The leak to the *Enquirer* had been a bad idea, and maybe he wasn't thinking clearly, but he was mad. He had been affected by the experience, too, and our marriage was suffering.

"I can't believe he would do this to Scott," Jackie went on. "We are terribly disappointed in him."

I didn't say anything.

"Anne?"

"I'm here."

"If anybody calls and asks you about Scott and the babysitter, deny it."

"Excuse me?" I wasn't sure I had heard her correctly. But if I had, she was asking me to lie.

"If anybody asks you—anyone at all—deny it."

Then I heard Lee's voice in the background—I believe she was on her cell, in his car—and he was more circumspect: "Just say you don't recall," he said. He said it loudly, so that I'd hear.

I hung up. That was it: I was going to have to separate myself from Jackie. Blood is thicker than water, but there's a limit.

Ironically, this wasn't the end of the babysitter story. By this time, Lorraine had found full-time work at Tommy's day care center, thanks in part to our recommendation. Shortly after the article appeared in the *Enquirer*, we were told that our son was no longer welcome.

I was very upset, but nowhere near as upset as Tim.

"Don't you wish your family had never found you?" he asked.

I didn't even know how to respond to that.

• • •

Not everyone on Jackie's side of the family was behind Scott. Two of his young cousins were absolutely floored by the tragedy. They told me that many years earlier, when Scott was in college in Arizona, he'd gotten a girl pregnant. Somehow he persuaded the girl to get an abortion, and when it was all over Scott came home to Jackie and Lee. He never went back.

When I became a mother, I read a few parenting books so that I could work on becoming the best mother I could be. I remembered reading something about the importance of teaching children not to run away from problems, to take responsibility for themselves.

Children whose parents constantly make excuses for their children's bad behavior can grow up to be reckless, irresponsible adults.

I wondered if Scott was living proof of that theory.

The second thing the cousins told me about was far more disturbing than the first. They said that Scott had been investigated in connection with the disappearance of Kristin Smart, a nineteen-year-old student at California Polytechnic, in San Luis Obispo. She disappeared on May 25, 1996, a year before I reconnected with Jackie and Scott, and around the same time that Laci Rocha graduated from Cal Poly.

"Who told you this?" I asked.

"We heard the rumors."

"Was he actually questioned?"

"Maybe not questioned, but someone said that he'd met her and that maybe they were even in a class together."

I hoped this wasn't true. If it was, and if Scott had actually been questioned, I'm sure the police had already made the connection, and they would probably be using it against him.

Now everywhere I looked I saw things that could be construed as evidence against Scott. When an article about the case appeared in *People* magazine, one of many, there was a photograph that showed Scott and Laci's dining table, set for Christmas Eve dinner. The article suggested that Laci had set it herself, shortly before she disappeared, but when I took a closer look I didn't think that was the case. Laci was a real stickler for detail, and she excelled at it. From what I could see, the table setting wasn't up to her usual high standards. The linens, the place settings, the silverware, the glasses, the flowers—none of it looked quite right. I wondered if perhaps Scott had set the table after the fact.

* * *

Scott wasn't setting any tables these days, but he kept writing me. He described the daily tedium, the bad food, his noisy fellow inmates, and a magazine called *Fine Homebuilding* that he seemed to find endlessly entertaining. He even wrote bad jokes: "Did you hear about the blonde who was bragging about having finished the jigsaw puzzle? The box said two to three years but it only took her one."

I wrote back dutifully—mundane things about the kids, Ryan's school, the weather, and the new neighbors—but he was always ahead of me.

"Sister Anne," he began in one letter and then went on to note that the phrase had a "conventish ring" to it.

In another, he wrote that he was deeply influenced by my letters. At first I thought he meant he took comfort in them, but then I realized he was talking about the style of my handwriting, the shape of each letter, and the general presentation. He noted that the letters were a "positive force" in his life, and that he was working hard at emulating me.

I thought back to the day he returned from the P.O. box in Modesto with that stack of mail, including the death threat he was convinced was from the Rochas. I remembered how he had commented about the penmanship. "Look at this nice handwriting. . . . I wish I could write like that."

What could all this mean? Scott was focusing on style, not substance. His life was being threatened—he saw the words right there in black and white. But he didn't seem to hear them. His attention was elsewhere.

The next time Jackie called, she told me I should visit him. "There are only a few approved visitors on the list, and you're one of them. He very much wants to see you."

I went with Lee's daughter, Susan, Scott's half sister.

The Stanislaus County Jail is an old building, very dated. It's falling apart, actually. The glass is chipped in many places. There are broken tiles everywhere. It even smells old.

I was so tense and uncomfortable that I let Susan lead the way, and I hardly remember how we got there. All I know is that we found ourselves standing in a murky, depressing waiting room, in front of one of the few cubicles that had a working telephone, and that I could feel my heart beating wildly in my chest.

I kept trying to calm myself down with silly thoughts. *Why, this is just like in all those movies I've seen!* I tried to recall some movies I'd seen that featured prison visiting rooms, but none came to mind.

Then a door opened—far, far away, it seemed, on the other side of the bulletproof glass—and Scott walked in, with a deputy close behind. He was wearing a reddish-orange jumpsuit, the kind I think they call a carrot suit, and his hands were cuffed and linked to the chain that circled his waist, like a belt. I thought the deputy was going to remove the cuffs, but he didn't, and Scott walked over, trying to smile, and sat down. It was hard for him to reach the phone because the chains didn't have much play. He had to bend forward to grab it, and he had to lift it off the receiver, as his chains rattled. When he sat down, he was forced to twist his entire body and cock his head at an odd angle to press it to his ear.

Susan talked to him first. I couldn't hear his end of the conversation, so I just sat there trying not to look like I was going to scream. She talked about her kids, and about the family, and how everyone was thinking of him and asked whether he needed anything.

It was horrible to see him like that. I thought back to the last time I'd seen him, which was right after we returned from that trip to San Diego. He had changed and showered and left without telling me where he was going. I remembered thinking how wholesome he had looked. Now he didn't look so wholesome.

When Susan handed me the phone, I didn't know what to say. I looked at him through the grimy glass and hoped I was smiling.

"Hey, Sis."

"Hey."

"What have you been up to?" he asked.

"You're missing some real good episodes of *Murder, She Wrote.*"

He cracked up. I mean, *really* cracked up. I guess it broke the tension. The rest of the conversation was about kids, the family, and everyone's general health, and it ended with a promise to send him books and more magazines. Not a word about Laci and Conner. Not a word about life in prison. Not a word about guilt or innocence.

That's all I remember from inside the prison. Outside was a different story, however. Susan and I had just left the building, and we were making our way across the parking lot, toward the car, when she snapped, "I can't believe you said that!"

"What?"

"About *Murder, She Wrote!*"

"We used to watch that together."

"I don't care. He's in *prison*. They think he's a murderer. What were you thinking?"

I just let it drop. I knew what I was thinking. I was thinking it would be a good idea to keep it light. And that's what I'd done. I wanted to see Scott smile, and I got more than I bargained for. He had laughed: a big, happy, laugh—a genuine moment of levity. I thought that was a good thing, no matter what Susan said.

• • •

Scott kept writing, and in early July he sent me birthday wishes. "You're not one of those people who will celebrate her thirty-ninth birthday for seven years now, are you?" he asked. "You will just have to face the fact."

I wrote back, and my letters were so mundane that I was

ashamed of them. Did he really want to know that Ryan, at age three, was still in the throes of the Terrible Twos?

His next letter was actually forwarded to me by Jackie, but it was meant for all the people he loved. Jackie had typed his words into her computer, and e-mailed the letter to various members of the family, including me. Scott began by saying that he would spare us the details of his days behind bars, which were terribly monotonous, one running into the next, then added that he had to be cautious because "whatever I communicate is subject to the deceitful and misguided eyes of those who have put me here and caused my family so much pain. . . ." He talked about some of the books he'd been reading and noted that they had a common theme: the outdoors, adventure. They included *Alaska, Nothing Else Like It on Earth; Undaunted Courage;* and—the one he was in the process of tackling—*Travels with Charley.* He complained about nightmares, although he didn't go into detail, and said he'd been moved to a new, quieter cell, farther away from the drunk tank. He closed with, "The true lifeline is the telephone and your visits."

• • •

For a long time, nothing happened. The media struggled to keep the story alive, but there was little to report. Scott was in prison. The lawyers were reviewing the material. The investigators were still putting together pieces of the puzzle.

I lived in fear that I would be called to testify, but I wasn't.

On November 18, 2003, following an eleven-day preliminary hearing, Scott was ordered to stand trial for the murders of his wife and unborn child.

The Christmas that followed wasn't exactly the best Christmas of our lives.

*   *   *

At the end of January 2004, I got a very bizarre letter from Scott. He had already spent nine months behind bars, and I wondered what it was doing to him. The letter was either a sign of his mental deterioration or a stab at serious writing. "The environment is sterile with a concrete floor, stainless steel fixtures and sliver of deeply tinted window which changes from black as pitch to battleship gray through the cycle of the sun," he wrote. "An attempt to look through it yields only your reflection. I wonder if even its change of hue is due only to the changes of the interior lighting conditions. . . .

"I will take this time to humanize this cell with my pictures of Laci and the rest of our family. A photograph from your wedding reception hangs above the scared [sic] desk."

The following month, and again in March, I was subpoenaed and told I might be called upon to testify for the defense. I was horrified. I didn't want to testify. I was so confused by this point that I began to wonder whether I might make a better witness for the prosecution. I wasn't going to lie on the stand, even for my brother. I was almost certain I would fall apart under cross-examination. By some miracle, however, I was put off both times. It appeared that I would not be called.

After the danger passed, I went to visit Scott again. The trial had been moved to Redwood City, and he was now being held at the Maguire Correctional Facility. Jackie gave me some advice before I went. "You have to check in before visiting hours," she said. "You'll see people lining up. And listen, this is important: I want you to write Scott's name down on a piece of paper, and when the deputy asks who you're there to see, just give him the paper. You don't want to say his name out loud."

Before I went, I visited the jail's website and read through the long list of rules and regulations. You weren't permitted to take any personal items into the visiting room, not even your purse. You couldn't bring gifts for the inmate, not even books or magazines. The visits were limited to two per week, forty-five minutes in length. If you showed any disrespect to the staff, you would be escorted out of the facility and future visits might be revoked. They also had rules regarding children, noting that at certain hours there were volunteers present to help out. I imagined a young mother visiting her husband, trying not to fall apart, while her children, oblivious, played in a room off the lobby under the supervision of a complete stranger.

I went on my own this time. When I pulled into the parking lot, on Bradford Street, I could already see people moving toward the entrance. I parked and cut the engine and wrote Scott's name on a small piece of paper, just as Jackie had instructed me to do. I had a magazine with me, so I tucked the slip of paper between its pages. Then I got out of the car and approached the building. It had a white façade, with the words BRENDAN P. MAGUIRE CORRECTIONAL FACILITY etched into the stone in tall letters. The glass front doors were to the left, and I stepped through them and got in line.

I was pleased to see that this place was a huge improvement over the last one. It was a modern, clean building. There were three deputies behind bulletproof glass, tending to the visitors.

When it was my turn, I looked for the slip of paper and couldn't find it. I felt like an idiot. It had probably fallen to the ground in the parking lot.

"Who are you here to see?" the deputy asked me.

I took a moment. "Scott Peterson," I whispered.

"Who?" He couldn't hear me through the glass.

"Scott Peterson," I said, and this time *everyone* heard me. The entire room turned to stare at me.

"Are you on the list?"

"Yes," I said.

"Driver's license?"

I fished out my license and gave it to him, and he checked me against the list of approved visitors then waved me through. People were still staring at me, making me feel as if *I'd* done something wrong. I tried to ignore them as I made my way through the metal detectors.

When I emerged on the other side, I noticed that most of the visitors were being herded off toward the west side of the building, but an older women and I were sent in the opposite direction. She seemed to know what she was doing, so I followed her into the elevator and up to the third floor. We didn't talk. I looked at the numbers as the elevator climbed.

When the doors opened, we stepped outside. There were several heavy wooden doors on the far side of the corridor, leading to the various visiting rooms, with little windows you could see through, into the room itself. They had names like "East Visit 1," "East Visit 2," and so forth. It was clean and private and it was very quiet, mostly because we were the only two people on the floor.

"You have to let them know you're here," the woman explained, indicating an intercom on the wall. She could see how confused I was, and she went over and pressed the button and announced her son's name. Then she turned to me. "Who are you here to see, dear?"

"Scott Peterson," I told her. I guess she'd missed it downstairs.

The name seemed to give her a little jolt. She turned her attention back to the intercom and repeated it. "And Scott Peterson."

"Thank you," I said.

For a few seconds, we were both silent. Then curiosity got the better of her. "*The* Scott Peterson?" she asked.

"Yes," I said.

"Just wait here, dear," she said after a pause. "You can see the rooms if you stand here in the middle. When they bring him out, you just go on over."

"Thank you."

She made no further comment, and the silence bothered me. I wanted to make conversation, so I unthinkingly asked her what her son was in for. She said it was a home invasion. I didn't get it, and she saw the confusion on my face.

"Murder," she said.

That's when it hit me: We were in the maximum-security wing of the prison. "Does your son know Scott?" I asked.

"He's seen him," she said. "But I don't believe they've talked."

A moment later, she saw her son being led into one of the visiting rooms, and she smiled at me and wished me well and went off to see him. A split second after that, I turned and saw Scott being ushered into one of the other rooms. I hurried over, trying hard to smile. And I think I *was* smiling a little. He was wearing a prison jumpsuit, but the chains and the shackles were gone, which in and of itself was a relief.

We sat down simultaneously and picked up our respective phones.

"Hey, Sis," he said, and he had a big smile on his face.

"Hi," I said.

"How's it going?"

"Good. You?"

"Thanks for coming to see me."

At that moment, I caught sight of my reflection in the glass, almost superimposed on his face. It was eerie. Our faces fit together almost too well, and I was disturbed by the similarities.

"I'm such a klutz," he was saying. "I was hurrying up the stairs, and I tripped and lost my shoe. The guard had to wait for me. That's why I'm a couple of minutes late."

"Are you okay?"

He said he was fine. He had his own cell, and he was reading a lot, and nobody really bothered him much. There was something very flat about his delivery, an almost complete absence of inflection. He didn't express any feeling, and he didn't talk about his feelings, and because there was something almost subhuman about it I began to feel very uncomfortable. I didn't know what to talk to him about or what to ask him. I didn't want to say anything to upset him.

"I enjoy getting your letters," I said.

"I enjoy getting yours."

"Are you reading a lot?"

"Reading and sleeping. Plenty of time for both."

It was excruciating. Finally, I couldn't take anymore. "You must really miss Laci," I said.

And he looked at me, paused for a moment, and said one word: "Yeah."

That was it. *Yeah.* Completely devoid of emotion.

When I left, I was surprised at how casual and uneventful the visit had been. I don't know what I had expected, but I felt almost disappointed—as if I'd just had a conversation with a stranger at a bus stop. What's more, I felt useless. I realized I had done absolutely nothing for him. I imagined him going back to his cell, picking up a book, and falling asleep on his little mattress.

I visited him twice more. Jackie had gone to see him, which she was doing twice a week, and she told me that his spirits had been greatly buoyed by my visit. I had seen no evidence of that, but I wasn't going to argue.

The second visit was more of the same—we talked briefly about *Alaska,* a book he found engrossing—but there were long patches where I had to struggle to fill the silence. I kept reminding myself that this was my little brother in there, and that the human contact—just seeing me there, through the glass, and hearing my voice—was probably good for him.

The third visit was as quiet as the others, and I found it excruciating. Much as I hate to admit it, I was waiting for the visit to end, waiting for that telltale flicker of the lights that warns you your time is up, that the guard is on his way.

When it came, we were facing each other through the glass, the phones in our hands. Scott looked away suddenly, not wanting to meet my eyes. He was looking down, and a little to the right.

"You know I didn't kill my wife," he said.

Then he looked back up at me, as if to gauge my reaction, and a moment later the door behind him opened and the guard came through. Scott stood and turned his back and walked away without another word. I watched him until he was out of sight, watched until he and the guard slipped outside and the door swung shut behind them.

It was the first time he had proclaimed his innocence.

And I really, truly wanted to believe him.

The dinner table at the Petersons' house: Laci would never have set it so poorly.

CHAPTER
VIII

THE LIST

In early March, jury selection got under way in Scott's trial, and in a little under four weeks they had seated six men and six women.

One cloudy afternoon, a few days before the trial began, with the kids fast asleep and Tim not yet home from work, I found myself sitting on the couch, looking at old photographs. I'm not sure what had prompted this. Maybe I was feeling nostalgic. Maybe I thought I'd find some answers there. Maybe I was worried about the days ahead.

I hadn't looked at them in a long time, and many were still in their Photoworks envelopes. There were pictures of the Latham family reunion in La Jolla, including one of Laci and Scott. I happened to notice that Scott's wedding band was clearly visible.

I found a picture of me and Jackie doing the tourist thing in San Francisco, with the Golden Gate Bridge in the background. That had been a fun visit. She had come up for the weekend, and we'd gone out and done girl stuff. We had manicures and pedicures, and we had a long, leisurely lunch at Perry's, on Union Street.

There was a nice shot of my parents and me in a San Francisco restaurant, during one of their frequent visits, taken by a helpful waiter.

And there were several photographs taken during Laci's shower. There was a group shot, a shot of my mom and Jackie, and one of Scott and me at the tail end of the shower, shortly after he showed up to help Laci pack up her many gifts.

Those photographs had been taken on December 10, 2002. Two weeks later, Laci was gone.

I kept sifting through them, stirring up all sorts of memories. I found a shot of Scott and Laci at my wedding reception at the Top of the Mark, and another that just took my breath away. It was of Jackie with her four kids: Don, me, John, and Scott, her golden boy. . . . The two kids she had given up and the two she had kept.

More recently, there was a photograph of Jackie and Lee at Tommy's christening, on January 12, 2003, only a few weeks after Laci went missing. Scott was there, too, of course, holding Tommy.

Once again, I remembered what Lee had said to the rector that day, right after the service, his voice tight with emotion: "How does one get through it?"

I didn't know how anyone was going to get through this: not the Petersons, not the Rochas, not Scott himself.

• • •

On June 1, in Redwood City, the trial finally began. "Think back to 2002," Rick DiStaso, the prosecutor, said in his opening statement. "Sharon Rocha was preparing for a Christmas Eve dinner. Laci and Scott were coming over at six. Sharon had put out the presents and set the table. At 5:15 P.M. the phone rings. It's the defendant, the son-in-law. 'Mom, is Laci there?' he asks. 'No,' Sharon answered. 'She's not supposed to be here until six.' 'I came home after a drive,' Peterson said. 'I went into the backyard, and the dog was there with the leash.' 'No, she's not here. All day. Did you call her friends?' 'No I haven't,' Peterson replied. 'Call them, and call me back,' Sharon suggested. Peterson called again very quickly. 'I called back, and I'm not able to locate her. Laci's missing.' 'Did you check with the neighbors?' she asked. 'Laci might be delivering cookies.' 'No, I haven't,' he said. At that point, Sharon turned to her husband, Ron Grantski, and said: 'Something's wrong. Laci's missing.'"

DiStaso's ending was plainspoken and conclusive. "Ladies and gentlemen, this is a common sense case. At the end of this case, I'm going to ask you to find the defendant guilty of the murder of Laci Peterson, as well as the murder of his son, Conner."

Then it was Mark Geragos's turn. He said Scott was innocent—"stone cold innocent"—and that he intended to prove it. He contended that Laci had lived well beyond December 24, the night she was reported missing, and that baby Conner had been born alive. He said the crime had been perpetrated by transients, and that witnesses had seen Laci being shoved into a van. I had no idea that this was going to be part of the defense, and it threw me. I had been following the case as closely as possible, more closely than was good for me, and I was under the impression that there had been no truth to those rumors about the transients—that the van belonged a landscaper, and that no one was able to confirm the existence of a purple car with Confederate flags.

"This is a murder case, and there has to be evidence in a murder case," Geragos said. According to him, however, there was no evidence. As he put it, the police had "Zip. Nothing. Nada. Not a thing!"

· · ·

Then a terrible thing happened. I was told that the prosecution wanted to talk to me. I thought this was highly unusual—the trial was already under way—but it turned out to be fairly common. There's always a great deal of confusion before a big case, and no one ever has all their ducks in order. Potential witnesses tend to slip through the cracks, and I happened to be one of those potential witnesses.

I called Jackie, in a bit of a panic. "I don't know what they want from me," I said.

"I'll talk to Geragos," she said, "and I'll call you back."

I sat by the phone, a complete wreck, but she called within ten minutes. She said I should go down the night before I was scheduled to meet with the district attorney and that Geragos would arrange to have someone talk to me to prepare me.

About two weeks into the trial, I drove down to the Stanford Park Hotel, in Menlo Park. My mother met me there, so she could help with the kids, and Geragos sent one of his men over to prepare me for the next day. His name was Karl Jensen, and he was a retired FBI agent.

He asked me a number of questions, going back to the trip to Disneyland with Scott and Laci. He was particularly interested in the rented wheelchair because the prosecution was floating a theory that Laci had been battered and that she couldn't walk.

"I never even saw Laci in the wheelchair," I said. "But I saw Scott in it."

So much for that theory.

He asked me about some of the maternity clothes I had sent Laci, and he wanted to know if I had given her a pair of cream-colored Capri pants. I told him yes, that I thought those pants might have belonged to me, but I wasn't sure.

He reached into his briefcase, and I tensed up. I had heard that Laci had been found in those pants, and I was worried that he was going to show me a photograph. I made it clear that I didn't want to see any photographs. Mr. Jensen took his hand back out of his briefcase, and we moved on.

Before we were done, however, a call came through. The district attorney no longer wanted to see me; I wouldn't be testifying after all. I was hugely relieved. We finished our conversation, and I went to rejoin my mom.

In the morning, we packed up and got ready to leave. My mother said she was curious about the courthouse—it had become pretty notorious, and she wanted to have a look—so I called Jackie on her cell phone and asked if she could keep an eye out for my mother. I stayed with the kids, and my mother went over and chatted with Jackie and Lee for a while, amazed by the sheer number of people out there, including the battalions of reporters.

When she was on her way back, Jackie reached me on my cell and asked where we'd been staying. I told her we had spent the night at the Stanford Park Hotel, and she thought this was quite a coincidence. "We're doing an interview with Barbara Walters later today," she told me. "You want to stick around?"

"No," I said. "But thanks."

. . .

The Barbara Walters interview aired in July, and I watched it from home, with Tim.

"They had a very good marriage," Jackie said. "They backed each other up all the way. It was like it was them and we were all outsiders. They were totally dedicated to each other."

This wasn't quite the way she'd described the marriage to me. On several occasions, Jackie had indicated that the two were having problems. She never said the marriage was in trouble, but she'd given me cause to wonder, and she'd never described it in the glowing terms she was using now.

She talked about seeing Scott and Laci together four days before Laci disappeared, and how ecstatic they were as they patted Laci's belly, feeling for the baby's kicks.

When Barbara Walters noted that Scott wasn't showing much emotion, they were quick to defend him. They said Scott was just putting on a brave face, and that he often cried privately in front of them.

Lee said he knew Scott was innocent, that he didn't have it in him to kill Laci, and that the only time he'd ever seen him get a little mad was over a bad golf shot. As for the affair with Amber Frey, it was disappointing, he said, but not all that uncommon. "That's the reality of life. Men have affairs, women have affairs. . . . It certainly doesn't give motive for murder."

They said that Scott was holding up fairly well, given the circumstances, especially after a very dark period when he felt like giving up. His whole life had been devoted to Laci and the baby. It was still hard, of course, and sometimes they would try to bolster his spirits by talking about a more joyful past. "We try to keep him up, but things come up and when we mention it, then he starts weeping," Jackie said. "We just try to . . . remember the good things and nice times we had together. We'll always have those. No one can take those away from us."

When the interview was over, I didn't know what to think. Under the circumstances, I guess it didn't surprise me to hear Jackie painting an exaggerated portrait of a trouble-free marriage. But that didn't make it right, and it didn't make it true.

I wondered what I would have said if I'd actually been questioned by the district attorney. I know I wouldn't have lied. But telling the truth would have meant making a liar out of Jackie.

"What if there's a hung jury or a mistrial?" I asked Tim.

"What if there is?"

"That means they'd have to start all over again. I could get called for the second trial and get put on the stand."

"You could get called before that," he said. "For the rebuttal. Maybe they're saving you for that."

That was a frightening thought, especially since I remained so much in the dark. I *still* didn't know whose side I was on.

"You know I didn't kill my wife," Scott had told me.

In all honesty: No, I didn't know.

• • •

The next time I saw Dr. Tucker, I told her about the Barbara Walters interview and how conflicted I felt about Jackie's portrayal of the marriage. I said I understood Jackie's position—Scott was fighting for his life—but I found it hard to condone. I said it made me think about the meaning of justice and of those so-called Dream Teams of high-powered attorneys, and it was disheartening to think that justice didn't have all that much to do with right and wrong. I wasn't naive, I said—I have a pretty good idea of how the world operates—but this was personal.

"I loved Laci," I said. "Yet I still feel tremendous allegiance to my brother."

"I can hear how conflicted you are," Dr. Tucker said. "This really is a moral dilemma. You love him, and you don't want to see him get hurt."

"I really don't," I told her.

"Take a completely honest look at what it is you know and what it is you *want* to believe. It's not going to be helpful to you to live with a lie."

"So what should I do?"

"Tell yourself the truth," she said.

Before I left, Linda told me that I might want to try to organize my thoughts and put them down on paper. That day, I began to work on a list of things that were bothering me about the whole situation. The following is what I finally came up with—it isn't complete, and I'm no lawyer—but it shows how many things I was trying to process at that point:

1. On our last day at Disneyland, when Ryan went missing and everyone panicked, Scott stayed on his cell in his own world. Total disconnect.

2. While at Tommy's christening on January 12, 2003, Scott sat and held Tommy entire time and looked uncomfortable. Rector seemed to get bad feeling about Scott, like he knew something or wasn't buying it.

3. Scott upgraded his porn channel later that day.

4. In interviews with Gloria Gomez and Diane Sawyer, Scott said Laci knew about Amber. No way she knew he was having an affair! No way she would have put up with it.

5. On Ryan's third birthday, Scott stayed with us. He had just returned from his P.O. box in Modesto and had hate mail with him. There was a praying mantis on one, and another had a birthday cake picture with three candles and it said "Happy Birthday Ryan." This made me scared, and I do not know where it came from or how anyone else would know about Ryan's birthday. Also, there was a letter—the one he thought was from the Rocha family—that

was definitely a death threat. He seemed to be able to joke about it.

6. Scott partying, celebrating while Laci is missing. A lot of "carrying on" the entire time I was with him.

7. When he was at our house and the news came on, he watched and asked if he should get rid of his goatee. Did not seem to recognize how serious it was that he was a "person of interest."

8. Flirting with our babysitter. Made "flirtinis." Babysitter felt uncomfortable and left.

9. Jackie and Lee telling me that if asked about babysitter incident, I should just deny it or "not recall" it, suggesting to me that they didn't want anybody opening that can of worms.

10. The girl he got pregnant in Arizona—was this the reason he left college? The girl had an abortion; then Scott came home.

11. Scott often arrived in different cars. Was he switching cars to avoid being followed?

12. Scott borrowing the shovel up at Lake Arrowhead. He said, "I have a shovel I borrowed that I need to return." Is it possible he buried something?

13. Scott did not have money, according to Jackie. Yet he purchased items from REI and North Face outlets while here.

14. Appeared uninterested in search for Laci. I brought up several ideas/leads (from the news), but he had no direc-

tion/interest in them. I asked if there was anywhere anyone should be looking and brought out map of Modesto. He pointed to Mape's Ranch (?) like he was very annoyed with me. "Maybe there," he said.

15. I saw the table setting from the *People* magazine photograph and it looks like Scott set the table for Christmas Eve dinner. I have set a table with Laci at a Latham family reunion, and she sets the table correctly. The Christmas "crackers" are a finishing touch—not the only thing you put on a table. There is also no tablecloth and it looks absolutely not up to Laci's high standards of table setting (something she excelled at).

16. When I asked about his (new) hair color he said that it was bleached in the swimming pool up in Mammoth when he was there skiing.

17. Scott used alias—Cal, short for California, a name he said that he and Laci originally chose for Conner—to look at apartments for rent so that he didn't have to give his name. But that wasn't the name I heard (they wanted).

18. He left our house two to three times to go to Modesto to clean the pool and mow the lawn. He said he did not want the neighbors seeing the pool turning green. Did anyone check the pool for any evidence?

19. Chilling story about the overgrown cemetery in Mendocino. Made up? Possibly. On verge of confessing? Looked like it.

20. Two [of Scott's] cousins said he was investigated in connection with the disappearance of Kristin Smart, the girl from SLO (missing since 1996).

21. Cousins said somebody must have been helping Scott flee if there was all the stuff in the back of the car.

22. Scott tried to get help removing GPS device from truck. Very annoyed to be tracked at all.

23. Despite what Jackie said on television about Scott and Laci's "perfect marriage," on three separate occasions (before Laci disappeared) she told me Scott and Laci were having problems.

24. Scott claimed he'd had a delusion of speaking into the mirror at their house with Laci. He said this after I told him I had seen Sharon Rocha on the news saying she saw Laci on their couch. [Such visions] are apparently brought on by "extreme grief" or "extreme guilt."

25. Scott told me that he had another affair before Amber Frey, someone in SLO, and did not give a time when that one occurred. Also, had slept with someone (or two?) on an airplane flight. On that flight he said he "took turns" between two airplane bathrooms. I have no idea when this occurred and did not ask any other details.

26. In L.A., gay relatives took Scott barhopping, went to a gay bar. Scott said he was bummed that no one hit on him.

27. Every time there was a search in the bay, Scott's voice and reaction was more heightened, and he would say things like "They are wasting their time when they could be out looking for her," "Time would be better spent looking for her somewhere else." He was louder and more emotional when they were looking in the bay.

28. Drinks at the Ballast. At the bar, Scott pulled Mexican pesos from his pocket. When [Gordo] asked if he was going to Mexico sometime soon, Scott didn't respond.

29. Dinner at the SD Yacht Club with some of my friends. At 9:00 P.M. I told Scott that we had to get going, and he said that it was ridiculous—"Who cares?" I called home and said we would be late; kept getting "Who cares?" attitude from Scott, and finally said we had to leave about 10:30 or 11:00 P.M.

30. I was the first to call and let him know they found a body of a woman in the bay. He said "They'll find out it's not Laci, and they will keep looking for her."

31. When I said they'd found the body of a baby the day before, he said "What?! . . . That's terrible. Who would do such a thing?!" Seemed very disturbed and voice was loud and emotional again.

32. On April 17, 2003 Scott stayed at my parents' house in San Diego. When I asked him why he didn't go to the Lake Arrowhead house he said his car spun out. I don't believe he ever went there. I think he went straight to my parents' because he thought the police knew about the Lake Arrowhead house.

33. On last prison visit to Redwood, Scott waited till end of visit and said: "You know I didn't kill my wife." Couldn't look me in the eye, then checked for my reaction.

When all was said and done, the big one, for me, was the swimming pool. I kept thinking of Laci, slipping into the pool to take the weight off her aching back. It had become part of her routine. And I kept thinking of Scott, in the shadows of the house, watching her.

I will never know what, exactly, was wrong with their marriage. No marriage is perfect. I can't say whether theirs was inherently more or less troubled than most. Neither of them talked much about the marriage, but Laci couldn't stop talking about motherhood.

However, I almost never heard Scott say a single word about his son.

I'll go back to what I said earlier: I've read about men panicking when their wives become pregnant. They run off, have affairs, or, worse, leave them behind to fend for themselves. Maybe this isn't exactly the life they had in mind, the lives they thought they should be living, and they want out. Other men wait until they have three kids, and come to the same conclusion: *Things were supposed to turn out better than this.*

With Scott, it was hard to tell. I think he wanted out. Maybe Laci drove him crazy with her talking and her attention to detail and her love of flowers. But what could he do? She was eight months pregnant. If he left her, the golden boy would suddenly become a heartless bastard. And of course he'd be forced to support her and the child for the next eighteen years.

But if she died, tragically, that was different. Far different.

I also wondered about those cream-colored Capri pants that were reportedly clinging to Laci's body when it washed ashore. If Scott had drowned her in the pool, why was she wearing pants? Surely he wouldn't have taken the time to dress her lifeless body. And then it hit me: Maybe it wasn't that Scott just came across her in the pool and seized the moment. After all, by then the weather may have turned too cold for swimming. Maybe Scott had been planning this for a while. And maybe seeing her in the pool so often, bobbing there with her hands on her belly, had planted a seed in his head.

• • •

At the time, there were many things I didn't know, so they didn't even come into play. I didn't know that Scott had purchased a fishing boat shortly before Laci disappeared. I didn't know that one could use cement to make anchors. I didn't know that Scott had checked the tides in the San Francisco Bay on his computer. I didn't know that, weeks before Laci disappeared, he had told Amber Frey and her friend Shawn Sibley that he had "lost" his wife.

But even without that knowledge, I finished that list and came away convinced that Scott had murdered Laci.

If I hadn't known about Amber and the fishing boat and the cement and all the other details that emerged in the course of the trial, I would have thought he simply snapped one night. An opportunity presented itself, and he took advantage of it.

But now I think he'd been planning it for a while.

I think he was just waiting for the perfect night, and December 23 was perfect. He could have drowned Laci in the pool, held her down until she stopped kicking. Then all he had to do was put her in the back of his truck, cover her with a tarp, and wait till morning to drive her body to the Berkeley Marina.

It would have been as easy as that. And however he did it, this much seemed certain: He took her out into the strong bay currents, weighed her down with a cement anchor, and pushed her into the water.

I had gone from doubting his guilt to suspecting him of premeditated murder. If that seems like a leap, take another look at the list. And then think about all the damaging evidence that came out at the trial.

· · ·

I was back in Dr. Tucker's office. "I loved Laci," I told her. "My son helped me wrap gifts for Laci. I had told him all about his baby cousin, Conner.

"I want to do the right thing. Some day my children are going to grow up and ask me what happened, and I'm going to want them to know that I behaved morally, that I was a decent human being and did the right thing.

"Laci and Conner did not deserve this. The Rochas did not deserve this. And the Petersons did not deserve this."

Dr. Tucker told me that I was getting into areas that were well beyond her expertise. She suggested I contact an attorney.

I tried. I called two different lawyers, and neither of them seemed to know what I should do with the information. The second one asked me to come in and then told me it would cost me three hundred dollars an hour. I guess that was the price of justice. It was very frustrating. I began to wonder whether this was a sign, that maybe I wasn't meant to say anything at all.

I kept seeing Gloria Allred on TV, however, and I was impressed at how well she protected her client, Amber Frey. I reached her in Los Angeles, and we spoke briefly, and she asked if I could come down to see her.

Despite all Jackie's questionable behavior in the preceding months, I worried that meeting with Gloria was a betrayal of my birth mother. I had tried very hard to remain loyal, but after weighing the evidence against Scott I was convinced he'd murdered Laci. My little list wouldn't stand up in a court of law, true, but that wasn't the issue. I had to trust what I believed in my heart, and in my heart I believed Scott was guilty.

Gloria and her partner, Nathan Goldberg, sat patiently through my entire story. I told them how I had come to meet Jackie and the rest of the family, and how I'd slowly and cautiously forged wonderful relationships with them, especially with Scott and Laci. I told them that it had taken me a very long time to even accept the possibility of Scott's complicity in the murders of his wife and son, but that the fog had finally lifted.

I even told them how I thought Scott had murdered Laci, and why.

"I feel I am betraying this family, but I don't feel I have a choice."

When it was over, Gloria explained that I should think about sharing what I knew with the police. I had already met with Detective Grogan, of course, so the authorities were clearly aware of me. But that had been a long time ago, back in the days when I still believed Scott was innocent. At this point, given everything I'd learned since, I had a different story to tell.

Gloria asked me to think things over very carefully. "This new information could be very important to the case and to the cause of justice, and you need to factor that into your decision," she said. "And of course I don't have to tell you how much of an impact this could have on Jackie and that whole side of the family."

After we were done, I drove to the cabin in Lake Arrowhead, where my parents were staying, and told them about my meeting with Gloria. My father seemed concerned, and my mother was actually quite upset. They were worried about the ramifications. After all, Jackie was family.

Back in Berkeley, I told Tim what had happened, and I told him I was sorry. I didn't have to spell it out for him. He knew what I meant. For the longest time, I hadn't been able to get my head around the fact that my brother might be guilty, and it had almost destroyed our marriage.

He could have made me feel lousy about it, but he didn't. Instead, he took me in his arms and held me close.

Outside the courthouse in Redwood City, November 12, 2004

THE
VERDICT

On August 10, 2004, Amber Frey was called to the stand. I knew I was going to hear some very disturbing things about Scott—Gloria had been keeping me apprised of developments in the case—but I was in no way prepared for what came next.

Everyone knew Amber had had an affair with Scott—although perhaps "affair" is the wrong word, since she didn't know he was married—but few of us knew when and how she discovered the truth. As it turned out, the woman who had set them up on that first blind date, Shawn Sibley, later found out that Scott was married, and she confronted him. He had a pretty convincing answer for her, and he subsequently shared that answer with Amber.

As Amber recalled on the stand, "He said he had lied to me about ever being married, and he had stated that sometimes for himself, when people would ask, it was easier for him to say that he was not or never had been married."

"Did he tell you why he had lied about being married?" the prosecutor asked her.

"That it was painful for him."

"Did you ask him or did he explain why it was painful for him to say he had been married?"

"Yes."

"What did the defendant tell you?"

"That he had lost his wife."

It was unreal. This was weeks before Laci went missing. I felt I'd stumbled into another dimension, a dimension where my reality made no sense.

I was riveted by the testimony, especially by the recordings of their phone conversations. "I'll be in Paris tomorrow," he told her a week after the murder. "I'm taking a flight from out in the country in Normandy, so I'll call you tomorrow." On the last day of the year—just a few hours before a candlelight vigil was being held for his missing wife in Modesto—he called Amber again. "I'm near the Eiffel Tower," Scott told Amber. "The New Year's celebration is unreal. The crowd is huge. . . ."

All my conversations with Scott came rushing back. How could I have believed a word he said?

· · ·

Jackie called me right after Amber's testimony, enraged. "What does that prove? That Scott had an affair with a bimbo! So what? There's no evidence against Scott. They have nothing."

I didn't want to upset her, but I couldn't control myself. "What about all those lies?" I asked cautiously. "About the Eiffel Tower and Normandy and all that?"

"Well, he's been all those places!" Jackie snapped.

Wow. She was in complete denial.

When we got off the phone, I sat there for a good twenty minutes, numb, unable to move, lost in thought. Then I picked up the phone and called Gloria. I told her to go ahead and contact the investigators, and to tell them that I would do whatever was asked of me. She got in touch with the right people, briefly filled them in on what I knew, and left it in their hands.

I did not hear from them, and, much as I hate to admit it, I was relieved.

. . .

Amber Frey continued to provide some of the most compelling testimony in the case. She explained that her growing suspicions about Scott eventually led her to discuss them with her friend Richard Byrd, who happened to be an officer with the Fresno Police Department. When the truth emerged, he told her she needed to call the Modesto police, and she called them right away.

To me, the most chilling part of her testimony was the day she confronted Scott, forcing him to tell her the truth about Laci. It was almost too painful to bear. That was my brother's voice on those tapes, and the woman he was talking about was not only his wife but also my close friend.

"The girl I'm married to—her name is Laci," Scott said. "She disappeared just before Christmas. For the past two weeks I've been in Modesto with her family and mine and searching for her."

"You've been calling—having conversations with me when all this is happening?"

"Yeah."

"Really? Isn't that a little twisted, Scott?"

"It is."

"Well, at least you agree with me there," she said.

The prosecution also gave Amber a chance to clarify the nature of her relationship with Scott. "Before Richard Byrd had passed that information on to you," she was asked, "did you know the defendant was married?"

"No."

"Did you know that he had a wife by the name of Laci?"

"No."

"Did you know that his wife was missing?"

"No."

The court also listened to a portion of Amber's February 19 conversation with Scott.

"I think right now, for me, Scott, and really everything that has happened in the past fifty-plus days for myself and—and the family and you and everything that's going on right now . . . I think it would be best if you and I didn't talk anymore until there's resolution in this whole . . ."

"Yeah. I agree with that."

"Good. Good."

"You're right."

It was almost impossible to believe that this was my brother. I was simultaneously repelled by, and attracted to, every little detail. I would watch the news after putting the kids to bed, trying to connect those dates and times to the dates and times Scott had been in my company and under my roof.

I realized that Scott had been at my house on the day Amber decided to end all communication with him, and I remembered that he'd shown up in the kitchen early in the morning, looking a little blue.

And I was upset when I heard him inviting her up to the cabin in Lake Arrowhead. That was my parents' cabin. I hadn't made it available to him so that he could have trysts there with his girlfriend.

I also wondered about the few times one could hear other voices on the recordings, in the background. Amber asked about those voices from time to time, and I wondered whether one of them was mine.

And I thought back to that last day at Disneyland, when Scott was sitting in the wheelchair, in Jackie's suite, on his cell phone, ignoring the unfolding drama over my missing son—the drama that ended happily a scant thirty seconds later, when I found him on the balcony.

There was also a point where Amber asked Scott whether Laci had known about the relationship, a question that had been on the minds of a great many people, including Diane Sawyer and Gloria Gomez.

"I'm saying now, was Laci aware of the situation about me?"

"Yes," Scott replied.

"She was?"

"Yeah."

"Really? How did she respond about it?"

"Fine."

"Fine?"

"Yeah."

"An eight-month pregnant woman fine about another woman?!"

"You don't know all the facts, Amber. You don't know all the facts."

I listened to those tapes, and I read the transcripts online, and all I could think was, *Who is that guy?*

• • •

On September 6, Jackie dropped me a line. "Have you written to Scott lately? He always asks about you when I see him."

I hadn't written to Scott lately. I was too focused on the trial. I was particularly intrigued by the testimony of Detective Grogan, who had questioned me on the phone so many months ago. He told the court that there were plenty of clues early in the case that led detectives to the San Francisco Bay. He said Scott had never told anyone in his family about the purchase of the boat and noted that the police had found cement debris on the floor of the warehouse where the boat was stored. He also said Scott had told investigators that his fishing trip on December 24 had been an unplanned, last-minute decision, but the fishing license had been purchased four days before the trip. Police also found it a little odd that Scott paid cash for the boat and that he had never bothered to register it.

There was also the issue of the alibi, which seemed to have changed. Apparently, Scott told a neighbor that he was out golfing when Laci had disappeared, but changed his story when questioned by the police. Grogan said he thought that Scott's plan had been to say he was golfing and that he had never told anyone about the boat because he didn't want them to know it existed.

Grogan also said that on February 18 detectives searching Scott and Laci's house found two large duffel bags by the door. One of the bags contained more than two thousand dollars in cash, a bottle of wine, and Scott's wedding ring.

I kept racking my brain, trying to remember if I'd seen him that day. I knew I'd seen him the following morning, when Amber Frey broke off all communication with him, but I couldn't remember if he'd been around the previous day.

Other clues included the fact that a police dog had picked up Laci's scent at the Berkeley Marina, that Scott had been using the wrong kind of fishing tackle, and that a boat tarp was discovered in the shed at his house.

In early October, almost immediately after the prosecution wrapped up its case, Gloria called to tell me that they wanted to talk to me. It had taken them a while, but I'd been bracing myself for something like this, and—nervous as I felt—I was prepared.

I drove down to Redwood City and checked in with Gloria, and we went off and met with one of the prosecutors, Birgit Fladager, in Gloria's hotel room. She brought Detective Grogan with her.

Ms. Fladager said she had been given to understand that I had some information that might be of some importance to the case, and with my permission she turned on a tape recorder and began to ask me questions. I had my list in my head, and I tried to walk her and the detective through each and every point, but I was a little flustered and I simply couldn't remember everything.

When they left, I felt awful—as if I hadn't done enough. But Gloria told me I had done just fine. She explained that they were preparing me as a rebuttal witness, but in the end—once again—I wasn't called. There was no rebuttal. Apparently, the prosecutor didn't think that Geragos had put on much of a defense, so he had nothing to rebut.

Now that I didn't have to worry about being put on the stand, I began to worry about Scott. "What's going to happen to him?" I asked Gloria.

"He could get the death penalty," she said.

"I don't believe in the death penalty," I said. "I think it's barbaric. I don't know what to do."

"There's nothing you can do," she said.

. . .

On October 12, as the defense dragged on, Jackie dropped me another line. "If you have any time you would like to spend with me next weekend, I will be here alone again." She said there was an amusement park near Modesto, as well as a pumpkin farm, which she knew the kids would like, and suggested that we might consider taking them for a swim at the Marriott pool.

It was hard to see her trying to be just a regular mother and grandmother. I guess you do what you can to make the center hold.

Jackie ended the letter with a suggestion: "Don't watch any talk shows or local news."

On October 26, the defense rested, and two days later I got an e-mail from Jackie. "Scott asked if I'd seen you lately when I visited this week. Do you still write?"

She also asked me what we were doing for Halloween, and when I replied, a few days later, I wrote the following:

Dear Jackie,

Yes, we're ready for Halloween. Somehow we have never been to the 'greatest street in Berkeley' for Halloween. . . . So this year we are going to walk that street. The boys are ready and very excited. Ryan has a birthday party to go to today. . . . We are trying to find a kindergarten for Ryan and the deadline is December 10 for most schools. . . . Tommy is on top of the table with crayons. I have to run.

Love Anne

On November 1, following twenty-three weeks of testimony, Rick DiStaso delivered his closing arguments. "He wants to live the rich, successful, freewheeling bachelor life," he said, painting a portrait of Scott's state of mind in the weeks before the murder. "He can't do that when he's paying child support, alimony and everything else. . . . He didn't want to be tied to this kid the rest of his life. He didn't want to be tied to Laci for the rest of his life. So he killed her."

Geragos opted for an ironic approach: "Do you all hate him?" he asked the jurors, indicating Scott. "That's the sum total of what we heard yesterday. Four hours about he's the biggest jerk to walk the face of the earth; he's the biggest liar to walk the face of the earth. You should hate him; you should hate him; you should hate him. Don't bother with the five months' worth of evidence."

On November 3, jury deliberations got under way, and nine days later—despite a few blips—they returned with a verdict.

Scott was found guilty on two counts of murder: the first-degree murder of his wife, Laci, and the second-degree murder of the fetus she was carrying, a little boy named Conner, a little boy who would never see the light of day.

• • •

As the time for the penalty phase drew near, Jackie called me, asking me to take the stand and tell the jurors about Scott. "You knew him so well. You two were so close. You can tell them all sorts of wonderful things about him."

I could have said some wonderful things about him, yes, but they would have been lies. That Scott was gone. Maybe he had never existed. The things I could tell them now would only hurt him.

"I can't do it, Jackie. I'm sorry."

She kept calling, trying to persuade me to testify. This was our one chance to avoid the death penalty, she said. Wouldn't I reconsider? There was a psychologist on the defense team who would be glad to talk to me. So many people were coming forward on his behalf. Relatives, friends, neighbors, even an old lady whose tire he once changed on his way to work. Didn't I want to be part of that? Didn't I want to tell the world how wonderful he was?

No, I didn't. I no longer thought he was so wonderful.

"I'm sorry," I said. "I can't."

"Don't you want to save his life?"

I didn't answer. She called again later in the day, and again the next day, but I didn't return her calls.

• • •

Laci's side of the family spoke to the jurors first.

"She gave me a picture of the sonogram," Sharon Rocha said,

fighting tears. "It's the only picture I have of the baby, and it was taken on December 14. The next day, December 15, was the last day I saw her."

Laci's stepfather, Ron Grantski, also spoke, as did Laci's sister Amy and her brother Brent. "I miss her very much," Brent said. "I try to remember the good memories we have of each other, but they're overshadowed all the time by how she died . . . and maybe her knowing who did it. I don't think I've ever heard her be more excited than the day she called me up to tell me she was pregnant. She was going to be a great mother."

It was gut-wrenching. These people had lost a beloved member of their family, and now they were trying to convince the jurors that the man who had taken them from her, my brother Scott, should be put to death. And when they were done, Scott's side of the family would try to convince them to spare his life. The more one thought about the concept of justice, the more confusing it seemed.

Lee was the first to speak about Scott. "He was sunny, motivated, always took care of business, always had a direction," he said. "I love him very much. I have great respect for him and all these wonderful memories about him as a little guy growing up. . . . He woke up smiling and went to bed smiling."

Then it was Jackie's turn. "If you were to take Scott away from us," she said, "we would lose a whole family. It would be like Laci never existed."

Some of the newspaper reports said she looked very frail, and that at times it was almost impossible to understand her because she was crying so hard. "He's an exceptional young man, and he's my son," she went on. "I know he's not perfect. . . . But he is genuinely a loving, caring, nurturing, kind, gentle person."

I remember what she had told me after his arrest, repeatedly and with such ferocity: *Scott is not an evil person.*

And I remembered what Scott himself had told Amber on one of the tapes. "I am not an evil person," he insisted.

"You're not an evil person?" Amber echoed.

"I am not," Scott had replied. "I would never hurt anyone."

On December 13, 2004, the jury recommended that Scott be executed for his crimes.

ONE FINAL VISIT

On Sunday, November 21, I received another e-mail from Jackie. "We just got back from visiting Scott," she wrote. "He is so brave it breaks my heart seeing him in there. My regret is that I will probably be dead by the time he gets out of that hellhole." The note ends with, "We are survivors so somehow we will all get through this so please try to stay positive and don't be too sad. I love you. Jackie."

I didn't respond. For the next couple of months I tended to my family, and I worked on repairing the damage that the previous two years had done to my marriage. Tim and I began to find our way back. And Tommy was finally getting potty trained.

I tried not to think about Scott, but it was hard. I found myself thinking about him almost incessantly, obsessing, in fact, trying to figure out how it had come to that. When someone commits a horrible crime, we often refer to him as a monster. This helps us separate him from the rest of us and tells us that we aren't monsters—that we aren't capable of that type of behavior. But Scott wasn't a monster. He was a human being who had done something monstrous. By his actions, he had separated himself from those of us who don't do monstrous things.

Scott was very much like you and me. Sadly, he was more like me. He was my brother. The thought that we might share a similar genetic flaw kept me up at night, but sleeplessness gave me no answers.

I did a little research on this. I was concerned about bloodlines: Whatever was inside Scott—was it inside me, too? I discovered that most specialists believe that tendencies like Scott's are behavioral, not hereditary, although certain experts argue that some "flaw" has to exist in the individual for such problems to take root. I was suddenly reminded of the Parable of the Sower, and of what Scott had said to Amber: "I need to get some good soil for us." Maybe Scott knew there was something rotten inside him. Maybe the golden boy—the boy who could do no wrong, the boy who had never really been held accountable for much of anything—was trying to run away from his own darker self.

All of that was reassuring.

But there was another issue: guilt. I kept asking myself if I could have done something to save Laci and Conner. In retrospect, I realize there was never any hint of the horror to come. And, as I'd read in the course of my research, that type of behavior is usually spotted only after the fact. Hence the old clichés: "He was such a quiet person. He wouldn't hurt a fly." Or: "She was the sweetest, friendliest neighbor we ever had. All of us are in shock."

Later, Dr. Tucker assured me there was nothing anyone could have done to change the outcome. Laci was not a battered woman who kept going back to her abusive husband. She was a young wife who was looking forward to motherhood, and there had never been even a *hint* of trouble in their home.

• • •

Early this year, not having heard from Jackie, and feeling badly for her, I called and left a message. "It's me," I said. "Anne. Just checking up on you. Wanted to know how you were doing."

A week later, she phoned back and plunged right in: "So I hear you think Scott is guilty?"

"I don't know what to say, Jackie," I replied, stumped. "Things just aren't adding up for me. I'm sorry."

"That makes me very sad," she said. "I'm very disappointed in you, the whole family is disappointed in you, and of course your brother Scott is extremely disappointed in you."

By the time I got off the phone, I was crying.

• • •

Who could I talk to? This had been going on for years, and nobody really knew the whole story. I can't even begin to count the number of times I wanted to pick up the phone to call Sharon Rocha to tell her how sorry I was and to let her know how much my all-too-brief friendship with her daughter had meant to me. But I couldn't do it.

I guess a more courageous woman might have managed it, but I was afraid of rejection. It's that whole adopted-kid mentality: What if I make contact and they want nothing to do with me? How would I survive that?

For two years I couldn't talk to anyone. Not the Rochas because I was afraid they'd see me as the enemy. Not the reporters who showed up at our house because Scott was in the middle of a trial, fighting for his life. And not the prosecutors, who only became aware of the extent of what I knew when the trial was winding down.

When I finally spoke to Gloria and Nathan, trying to figure out what to do, trying to process all of this information, I realized that I had lived through an amazing experience. My mother had given me away when I was a tiny, mewling infant, and more than thirty years later we had found each other. These were my blood relatives. I had been raised by the Gradys, whom I adored, but here I was, being embraced by the Lathams and the Petersons.

There were so many of them, but the one I grew closest to was Scott.

. . .

At long last, I told Gloria I wanted to write a book about the experience. I said I wanted to write something that my kids could read when they were older, so they'd know what had happened and know what part I had played. I wanted to write something honest, a book about family and love and loss.

It would be tempting to say that I wrote this book for Laci, or for her mother, and in part I'm sure I did. But I also wrote it for me. I wanted to tell my story, my way, in my own words, and I've told it here, and now I'm ready to move on.

. . .

Toward the end of January, I spent a few days in Los Angeles, working on the book. On Tuesday, January 25, I began the long drive home. Three hours into the trip, however, I was too exhausted to continue, so I spent the night in a hotel. I called Tim and told him I'd be home the following morning.

I woke shortly before 6:00 A.M. to a gray, overcast day, grabbed a muffin and coffee, then climbed into my car for the rest of the drive north. Once again, I found myself obsessing about Scott. It had been a year since I'd last seen him, at the Maguire Correctional Facility in Redwood City. He was still there, waiting for his formal sentencing, which had just been rescheduled for Friday, March 11. The judge in the case, Alfred A. Delucchi, has the option of reducing

Scott's death sentence to life in prison, but no one thinks that is very likely.

As I made my way north, I realized I was never going to see Scott again. I was no longer part of that family, I knew I'd probably never make the trip to San Quentin, and I had a feeling that Scott would never talk to me again after reading what I've written here.

So I decided to go see him one last time.

In all honesty, I think a small part of me—a very small part of me—still wanted to believe that he hadn't done it. I guess I was hoping for a miracle. Maybe he'd say something that would convince me of his innocence, and I could do something with the information.

I took Interstate 5 North to CA-152, and when I reached Pacheco Pass I merged onto the 101 North. Fifty miles later, I got off at Whipple Avenue and made my way to Bradford Street.

It was raining pretty hard by the time I pulled into the lot, and there was a flash of lightning in the distance. I hoped this wasn't some kind of sign.

I wrote Scott's name on a piece of paper, got out of my car, and hurried through the rain to the glass front doors.

The place hadn't changed at all. There were three deputies behind that familiar pane of bulletproof glass. I walked up to the first one I saw—a woman.

"Who are you here to see?" she asked me.

I slipped the paper and my driver's license through the slot.

"Oh," she said.

The deputy next to her, curious, looked over her shoulder to see who I was visiting. He looked up at me, eyes wide.

"Are you on the list?" the female deputy asked.

"I believe so," I said.

She took a look at her computer. It was a very short list—Jackie,

Lee, Uncle Patrick, a few other Petersons, a Latham or two, and me, Anne E. Bird—and she signed me in. I thanked her and moved off, and I heard the deputy next to her say, "That's a new one."

It was early yet. I had made the trip from my hotel in less than three hours, and it was only 9:20, a full forty minutes before they'd let us in. There were a number of people loitering in the lobby, and a wiry man with dozens of little cuts on his face kept running around asking people for cigarettes. He reminded me of a ferret.

I went back to my car to wait, and for a while I began to wonder whether this had been such a good idea. Knowing what I knew now, how would it affect me?

"You know I didn't kill my wife."

That was the last thing he'd ever said to me.

• • •

A few minutes before ten, with the rain tapering off, I went back to the building and made my way through the metal detector then turned toward the elevator. Only one other visitor joined me in the maximum-security wing, but he got off on the second floor. I realized that the men in maximum didn't get many visitors.

When I reached the third floor, I got out and buzzed the intercom. A voice answered, "Yes?"

"I'm here to see Scott Peterson," I said.

I waited a few minutes, then a few minutes more. He didn't come. Then the intercom squawked: A voice told me he was in Number 5. I moved down the corridor and through the heavy door. As I approached, I saw Scott through the glass. He had his back to me, and seemed somehow broader. When he turned to face me, he was still rubbing his wrists—the shackles had just been removed—and I was momentarily thrown by his outfit. It kind of took my breath away. It was a padded, sleeveless suit, knee length, almost like a dress, and his arms and legs exposed. It looked as if it were made of Kevlar, but it was green and very thick, and it seemed constructed of two large, bulky pieces that had been stuck together with Velcro at the shoulders.

I sat down and studied him through the glass, hoping he wouldn't see the shock on my face, then picked up the phone and waited for him to reach for his. "Scott," I said. "How are you?"

"You know," he said. "I lost my family sixteen months ago."

That was quite the greeting. I noticed his face now. He was still Scott, certainly, but he had two deep furrows above his cheekbones, and he looked gaunt, like someone who had lost too much weight too fast. His skin was very white from lack of sunlight. Just looking at him was hard; it made me sad.

Then I noticed his arms. They looked huge to me, too muscular, and they made him seem even less like Scott. He raised one of his muscled arms and brushed back his hair, and I noticed it was wet.

"I was sleeping," he said, and he looked embarrassed, almost sheepish. "They told me I had a visitor. I didn't have much time to get ready."

What follows may not be exactly word-for-word, but I believe it's close. I didn't record our conversation, and I was nervous and flustered, and when I got home later it wasn't easy to remember every detail. But I've tried to document it as honestly and accurately as possible.

"It's nice to see you," I said.

"How's Ryan? How's Tommy? They must be getting pretty big."

"Oh yeah. They're growing up fast. How are you? How are things? Are you holding up okay?"

Slowly, he began to tell me about his life at Maguire. He was the only Caucasian in the prison's maximum-security wing; the other inmates called him White Dude. The food was bad, he said, and he didn't get much "rec" time, but he really enjoyed reading. The family was keeping him into books, and he loved hardbacks, and it bothered him that he wouldn't be getting any hardbacks in San Quentin. They were off-limits there.

"When I leave, I'll be making a generous donation to the library here," he said. "I only wish these guys had more respect for books. They like to deface them. There's a gang in here that's got a thing about the number 13, and they always deface that chapter. I don't get it."

Scott had a little soul patch on his chin, nicely groomed, but his eyes looked sad and tired. He told me he'd been a trusty for a while because he'd done a good job mopping the floors, and for a while the guards had let him deliver meals. Then he lost the privilege, but he didn't tell me why. Instead he told me about a neo-Nazi guy who used slivers of soap to draw Swastikas on the walls, marking his territory, and he said the guards would laugh because all they had to do was wash them off with water. And he talked about the empty cell next to his, which turned out not to be empty at all, and how the inmate flipped out one day and stripped off his clothes and refused to return to the cell.

"He'd never talked before; that's why I thought the cell was empty. Now he was saying only one word, and he kept repeating it: 'No, no, no, no, no.' The guards thought it was funny: this guy, naked, refusing to go back to his cell. And I never even knew he was there.

"Mostly if there's a guy in the cell next to you, you can talk to each other through the air vents."

"What do you talk about?"

"Nothing. Mostly I just read and sleep."

"You got strong," I said.

"Yeah. I do push-ups on my toilet. If you don't do them, you fall in. So you get pretty motivated."

He saw me looking at his outfit, and I couldn't help myself. "What is that thing?"

"This suit? I think it's called a Ferguson or something. It's like a dress, isn't it?"

He said a doctor had come to see him right after the verdict was read, a psychiatrist. He was there to make sure that Scott wasn't suicidal. Apparently, this was based on some type of point system, and the points were tallied according to two specific criteria: the answers you supplied to a series of direct questions, and the nature of your crime. "You get X number of points for killing a member of your family, X points if children are involved, X points if it's a girlfriend—that kind of thing," Scott explained. "If you get too many points, you end up in one of these."

I didn't know what to say. I guess Scott had scored fairly high. I didn't want to ask him if he'd been feeling suicidal, but he saw it in my eyes.

"I didn't get that many points," he said. "I just didn't like some of the things the doctor said in his evaluation."

"How did you know what he said?" I asked. "How did you find out? Did he tell you?"

Scott shook his head, not answering. "So where were you that you came by to see me?" he asked.

"I was in San Diego. I went to see my parents to pick up their old computer for Ryan." That was true, as far as it went. I didn't think Scott needed to hear about the book I was writing—the other reason I'd come south.

Suddenly the speakers squawked, and a voice said, "Mental Health to Cell Seven." It sounded like the kind of announcement you might hear at an airport, and Scott seemed to find it amusing. It was the first time he'd smiled in the entire visit. "Flight 321 now departing for Orlando from Concourse C," he said, sounding like an announcer himself. He was still smiling. "That happens all the time," he explained.

"They also have this thing called ERT: The Emergency Response Team. They bring those guys in whenever anyone gets violent."

"Does that happen a lot?"

"Sometimes."

"But you're okay?"

"They leave me alone."

There was a lull in the conversation. I wanted to ask him why he had killed Laci and Conner, but I just couldn't bring myself to do it. I'm not sure he knew why he had done it, and—a few moments later—I found out how right I was. Scott didn't even entertain the thought. It wasn't part of his reality.

"I hear they pushed the sentencing back a couple of weeks," he said.

"Yeah," I said. "I just heard that myself."

"Once this goes to appeal, it'll be all right," he said.

I held my breath.

"I mean, this has been just ridiculous," he went on. "This entire thing has been a big waste of time."

I took a breath, but I didn't say anything.

"I mean, I know it'll take a while. These appeals can drag on. But San Quentin won't be so bad. It's pretty famous. It's an old, historical building, overlooking San Francisco. It'll be a wait, but you get more privileges in the long-term facilities."

He took a moment, pursing his lips as if lost in thought.

"I'm kind of upset about the books, though. I like hardbacks. I'm trying to read them as fast as I can because I can't take them with me to San Quentin."

I felt like screaming.

"Yeah," he said. "After the sentencing, they'll take me over to San Quentin. A whole SWAT Team will come out, and they'll drive up the interstate at a hundred miles an hour. But I'll get out. When it's all over, I'll get out.

"And I won't need much, either. By that time, I'll have been in a six-foot cell for a while, so what would I need? Just a little space. I wouldn't even mind if I had to sleep with a toilet next to my head; I do that now."

He smiled again. "Everything I need, I'll find right at Home Depot. Not much at all. I'm going to live a very simple life. Everything is going to work out fine, Sis.

"Don't worry about a thing. Everything is going to be all right."

• • •

I sat in the parking lot and cried for a while. Scott was going to be locked away for the rest of his life, and it wasn't registering. He thought it was temporary. I guess they all do. I guess that's how they survive.

I found my way back to the freeway and headed home. Tim and the boys were waiting for me.

Family. At the end of the day, all you have is your family.

Acknowledgments

I'd like to begin by thanking Gloria Allred, who was such a tremendous source of support, and her partner, Nathan Goldberg, who was there whenever I needed him. Nina, Bill—you guys are the greatest.

My thanks also go to Judith Regan and Cal Morgan, from ReganBooks, for giving me a chance to tell my story.

A special thanks to Pablo Fenjves, who helped me shape this harrowing experience into a book. I loved working with you.

A big hug to the entire Grady Family: Mom, Dad, Stephen, Susan, and Michael. You're the best. I love you guys. To my Grandmother Gwen and the entire Johnson clan, a big hug.

For the Bird and Finch families, my deepest gratitude. Thank you for seeing me through this. To my sisters-in-law, Carina, Laurie, and Karin, I can say only one thing: I am very lucky to have you in my life.

To Ted Rowlands: Thank you for protecting my privacy. It will not be forgotten.

To Dr. Toni Brayer and to Dr. Cynthia Point, thank you both for your many kindnesses. And to Norma Lambert MacLeod, thank you for me helping make the right choices

To my girlfriends, Amy, Buffy, Marjorie, Denise, Kristin, and Karen, and to "The Vortex," Greg, Andrew, Jack, and Jim, thank you all for being there for me. Your unwavering friendship got me through the roughest patches.

A special thanks to my friend Roberta, at Berenice, and to Karla—a real lifesaver.

Finally, to my husband Tim, thanks for seeing me through these battles. And to my boys, Ryan and Tommy: You guys are the best part of my life. I love you more than you can imagine.